GOD, WHERE ARE YOU?

GOD, WHERE ARE YOU?

By
Merrill F. Unger

with
Zola Levitt

MOODY PRESS
CHICAGO

© 1975 by
THE MOODY BIBLE INSTITUTE
OF CHICAGO

Formerly entitled:
God Is Waiting to Meet You

Unger, Merrill Frederick, 1909-
God is waiting to meet you
1. Apologetics—20th century. I. Levitt, Zola
joint author. II. Title.
BT1102.U53   239   75-14099
ISBN 0-8024-3021-X

All scripture quotations in this book, except those identified otherwise, are from the New American Standard Bible, © The Lockman Foundation, 1960, 1962, 1963, 1971, 1973.

Scripture quotations from *The Modern Language Bible: The New Berkeley Version in Modern English,* copyright © 1945, 1959, 1969 by Zondervan Publishing House, are used by permission.

The use of selected references from various versions of the Bible in this publication does not necessarily imply publisher endorsement of the versions in their entirety.

Printed in the United States of America

CONTENTS

1

THE TODAY SHOW

In today's world God is being made to disappear!

The big question is not about doctrine—whether God is this way or that way—but about whether He *is,* at all. And if He *is* worshiped, He is all too often embalmed in theoretical theology. He is no longer, for many millions of people, the exciting God of the Bible who can be readily contacted—the God of miracle and power who transforms lives. For these people God is simply not "living" anymore.

There was a time, however, when God was called "The Living God."

The Living God

The Living God was a God you could count on!

The nation of Israel thrilled to "the voice of the living God" speaking out of the midst of the fire at Sinai (Deu 5:26) and "the living God" could be depended on to deliver them (Jos 3:10).

Goliath, the mighty Philistine, had reason to regret his effrontery in defying the armies of "the living God" (1 Sa 17:26), as did the Assyrians who reproached "the living God" in Hezekiah's time (2 Ki

19:4). Our Lord Jesus Christ commended Simon Peter for his revelation from the Father when the disciple identified his Master as "the Son of the living God" (Mt 16:16).

The pagan Thessalonians turned from idol worship to serve the "living and true God" (1 Th 1:9) and joined the Church of Christ, which is "the church of the living God" (1 Ti 3:15). Christians have their consciences purged from dead works to serve "the living God" (Heb 9:14), since an evil heart of unbelief departs from "the living God" (Heb 3:12).

Aptly, the heavenly Zion is designated as the city of "the living God" (Heb 12:22).

It was fashionable among the pagans of antiquity (and some of modern times as well) to manufacture gods from wood and stone. Hence the psalmist differentiated these idols from the living God. The gods of the heathen, he pointed out, "have eyes, but do not see, hands, but do not feel, feet, but do not walk" (Ps 115:5-7).

More recently, gods are made from philosophies and ideas—made with brains instead of hands. This creates confusion since it is hard to be sure of the characteristics of any given god. Actually, the old idols offered certain advantages over the new ones. Since they were made of stone, everybody could easily come by the temple and see god—a reliable old statue.

Lately we've come to the final refinement—the ultimate "improvement" on the living God. He is now, to many people, pure fiction. He doesn't exist anymore.

A Lifeless Religion

It seems that God was laid to rest by religious people, or at least by theologians of a kind. The modernist-fundamentalist controversies of the 1920s and '30s led to critical attacks on Scripture and the authority of the Word of God in the '40s and '50s. In the '60s God's demise was declared complete.

And now, in the '70s, there are many replacements for the traditional God of the Bible. Devotees of transcendental meditation, worshipers of Satan, and do-it-yourself theologies have gained a widespread following.

Lifeless religion looks like a valid worship at first glance, since the mechanics of worship are often included. But it separates the practice of religion from its life performance. So long as the devotee attends to the ritual, which is sometimes fanatic in its observance, whatever else he does is perfectly excusable. Hypocritically, the devotee dons the garb of religion when worshiping and takes it off again to live the rest of his life.

And this activity, as a matter of fact, is the basic root of the term "hypocrite." The word comes from the Greek *hupokrites,* meaning an "actor" or "performer on a stage." Such a person plays a role in his religion. He does not present his real self; he puts on a show.

Our Master has never been fooled by hypocrisy.

Lifeless religion spawns an infectious hypocrisy, and turns off many would-be believers to true religion. The assumption is made that those worshiping the counterfeit are worshiping the original, and that they are typical representatives of Christ's Church. Teenagers flee Christ when they observe their parents worshiping on a Sunday-only basis, leading a double life. Many a husband or wife, who is a potential convert to the true God, is turned away by a Dr. Jekyll-Mr. Hyde spouse.

The home tends to put hypocrisy to the test. The true follower of Christ is a husband who leads with compassion, a wife and mother of obedience and gentleness, and children who obey their parents in the spirit of being glad to be alive. But when the husband is a tyrant, the wife a nag and the children idle and contentious, hypocrisy runs rampant.

Worshiping a dead god, by definition, forces one to put on a show. Since the god is admittedly ineffective, the worshiper must produce all the effects of the religion on his own.

It seems an incredibly bad alternative to the living God!

Secularism

Secularism deserves to be called a religion, or at least a dead religion, in our times. It has become an all-pervasive way of life, as developed in today's world.

Capitalism and free enterprise have generated prosperity, with many people situated so comfortably that they feel they have no need for God. The dollar, with all its fluctuations, has become one of the deities, as preoccupation with the things of time and the senses has replaced appreciation for the spiritual and eternal.

The poet William Wordsworth already in his day saw the danger of gross materialism dominating the minds of men so that they lose touch with nature:

> The world is too much with us; late and soon,
> Getting and spending, we lay waste our powers:
> Little we see in Nature that is ours;
> We have given our hearts away, a sordid boon!

The fine sonnet goes on to describe the inexplicable joys of nature and creation, and the poet concludes interestingly:

> —Great God! I'd rather be
> A pagan suckled in a creed outworn.
> So might I, standing on this pleasant lea,
> Have glimpses that would make me less forlorn;

The poet would rather have been a pagan than a materialist, and it's food for thought.

Of course, nature, God-created, must have more to offer than blind object-worship.

But like the polluted air that hangs over our cities, the spirit that concerns itself solely with the objects of this life poisons many. God is reduced to a figment of the imagination. What the Bible declares about the living God becomes pious drivel.

The present secularistic trend is a heavy fog that hangs over men, and they can no longer see the road in front of them. Many have lost their way altogether. They have pulled to the side of the road to wait for the fog to lift, but it won't lift by itself. Spiritual fog does not clear up on its own.

The Today Show, spiritually speaking, is not too encouraging. But it does offer one bright spot. It is pressing relentlessly upon man's attention the fact that he does not live "on bread alone, but on every word that proceeds out of the mouth of God" (Mt 4:4).

When man realizes how emaciated he has become from a diet of stones instead of bread and humanistic philosophical husks instead of God's Word, he will seek the true Bread of Life.

If you are hungry for something better, you can be assured that God has it. He has already provided an alternative, and He is waiting for you to reach out and accept the better way.

The remainder of this book will show you how to find the living God and a living faith.

2

GOD IS ALIVE TODAY

You have to give credit where it's due. The anti-God forces have done a thorough job of making God disappear.

Dead theology, lifeless religion, atheistic Communism and materialistic secularism have been very successful in removing God from the consciousness of a vast segment of the human race. Millions may well ask, "After all, is there really a God to meet?"

But the answer remains clear. Uniquely enough, God has never been more alive, more necessary, or more willing to be encountered than in today's world.

This is the unanimous and enthusiastic testimony of millions of people the world over who have given God a chance to encounter them—to actually enter their lives. They have come out of that fog of unbelief into the realm of faith. They have come to the realization that without faith it is impossible to please God (Heb 11:6).

They have made the phenomenal discovery that "he who comes to God must believe that He *is,* and that He is a rewarder of those who [diligently] seek Him" (Heb 11:6, Greek).

The fact of the matter is, *faith pleases God.* The first faltering step of faith will evoke tokens of His pleasure. The mists and misgivings of unbelief—the plague of the multitudes of today's faltering world—begin to dissipate at the very first instant of faith. Each succeeding step of faith becomes steadier and increases the visibility ahead.

Soon the path of faith becomes well defined and the fog clears. The sun breaks through and reveals the unobscured blue of an open heaven.

I can never forget my encounter with the magnificent mountains of the state of Washington. I went there for a summer pastorate during World War II, while I was a student at Dallas Theological Seminary. Texas cannot boast of mountains, so I was eager to experience the scenic beauty of the rugged northwest ranges.

Unfortunately I arrived during a siege of bad weather. A damp, cloudy spell lasted several weeks and draped the landscape in foggy gloom.

Despite the inclement weather I took daily walks through the countryside, growing accustomed to looking through the mist and seeing things with a short-range perspective. I had almost forgotten about the snowcapped mountains which were totally hidden in the overcast.

Then one day the mist and the clouds suddenly disappeared. It cleared up, all in a moment.

I was thunderstruck! There before my eyes was the snowy cone of Mount St. Helens, seeming incredibly near and looking like a huge pyramid of ice cream.

And farther off, the giant Mt. Ranier, king of American mountains, wrapped in sunlight and gleaming like a diamond against the intense blue of the sky.

I stood still in my tracks, totally caught up in this glory of the Creator reflected in His creation. Moses saw God in the bush that burned with fire and was not consumed (Ex 3:2). Well, that day I saw God's glory in the snowy splendor of Ranier and St. Helens, and I realized an important lesson from the experience. The mountains had been there all the time. I just couldn't see them until the mist and fog cleared up.

So it is with God, I thought. Near as hands and breath, but unseen by millions, hidden from their view by the mist and fog of dead religion and stifling secularism. God is there, too, in communist lands. Denials of His existence by dictators cannot do away with Him.

God knows His own, behind the Iron Curtain or the Bamboo Curtain or any other curtain drawn by men. He cares for His own behind prison bars. He sustains them in Siberia and the cruel jails of China.

Many of His choicest spirits who died in faith in these miserable lands have been welcomed home to heaven to receive the martyr's crown.

When men are prevented from seeing the mountains, they foolishly assume the mountains aren't there. But when the mist finally lifted, I found the mountains waiting.

And the view was worth the wait!

Personally Speaking

I *know* that God exists.

Though a billion people under communist control might ape their leaders and shout, "There is no God," I know better.

And though another billion may shout about dead gods or stone gods or paper gods (like money), I know better than they, too.

I know God exists because I have met Him. He has met me and I have met Him.

Not only that, but our introduction has been followed by a life-long friendship—a warm fellowship with intimate communication that has sweetened with the many years.

Can anyone tell me that my friend of almost a lifetime isn't real? Is God, with whom I have conversed daily for so many years, a figment of Merrill Unger's imagination? Have the many benefits I have received from this enduring friendship, and the many services I have rendered in it, been merely useless self-deluding exercises?

How about my wife and children? I have been with them many years, with the same joyous exchanges of services and benefits. Is anyone ready to tell me my wife and children do not exist?

I was fourteen when God met me. He knocked and I opened the door. He extended the gift of grace and I gratefully accepted it. It has been all that He said it would be, and the best is yet to come! He gave me eternal life and I received it.

What sort of God was He who met me? Was He really infinitely loving, merciful, and gracious as the Bible says? I have to say that He is. I have known God and I have read the Bible, and He is all of those things. Is He infinitely holy, pure and sinless? Again, yes. That's how I have found Him.

Then why would He have anything to do with me?

Well, I was hardly a seasoned criminal or even a really "bad" boy when I met God. But the contrast between me and my Friend was obviously very great. How could He have bothered with me?

Well, my sins had been taken care of. Two thousand years ago, Christ, the eternal Son and eternal Word of God, became incarnate, and He accepted *my* death sentence. When I believed, I received salvation and was made a fit companion for God.

The enormity of it staggered me then, and it still does now. I needed salvation; I knew that by the time I was fourteen. I needed it as much as the worst reprobate.

I think this is where many good people go wrong. They shut the door in God's face and fail to meet Him as He draws near, because they do not come with a need. They do not approach as lost sinners, but instead plead their own goodness or dutifulness or some other positive quality. Consequently they demonstrate no need for salvation and they do not receive it.

They do not come to grips with their lostness and guilt contrasted with the infinite holiness of God.

I remember the night when God saved me as if it were yesterday. The invitation was being given in the

little neighborhood chapel as the service was conclud-
ing. Conviction was upon my heart, as it had been
more than once previously, to respond to the preacher's call. I felt compelled to go to the altar and kneel,
and trust Jesus Christ as my Saviour.

But I had a good excuse not to. I was the organist.
After all, *someone* had to accompany the congregation as they sang. How could I get up?

I sang along in my heart as I played that night:

> Just as I am, without one plea,
> But that Thy blood was shed for me,
> And that Thou bids't me come to Thee,
> O Lamb of God, I come! I come!

In truth, I doubt if anyone can hear that grand old
hymn without feeling a compelling urge to approach
the Lord at once. And I was well aware that I was a
lost sinner, desperately in need of salvation.

Suddenly I was on my feet and heading toward the
altar!

I just got up! Right in the middle of the singing!
As I walked, somehow without embarrassment of any
kind, I heard the hymn going on without the accom-
paniment. The congregation sang strongly on their
own:

> Just as I am, and waiting not
> To rid my soul of one dark blot,
> To Thee whose blood can cleanse each spot,
> O Lamb of God, I come! I come!

I knelt at the altar and the preacher knelt with me.
As I prayed he explained in my ear the simple truths

of the Gospel. Jesus Christ died for sinners. Did I realize that I was a lost sinner and that Jesus had borne my sins in His body as He died on the cross? Did I accept Him as my sin-bearer and substitute?

As I believed the Gospel, the light of God flooded my soul. I arose from the altar of prayer a new creature in Christ. Old things had passed away. Behold, all things had become new. A new heart, a new life, a new song, a new hope, a new sense and purpose in life.

God had saved me.

Good News for You, Too!

I don't have to tell you that God is not the exclusive possession of organists or people who go to little chapels. Actually, the message of the apostle Paul to the intellectuals of ancient Greece fully applies today.

Paul visited Athens and spoke in the Areopagus where the local philosophers were accustomed to considering cosmic questions. He was ideally outfitted to address this particular crowd, having been reared in sophisticated Tarsus and being conversant with the ways of the studious Greeks. His Greek was excellent, of course, and he knew how to put his message in the terms of his audience.

His words ring with wonderful relevance today:

> The God who made the world and all it contains, who is Lord of heaven and earth, does not dwell in temples built by human hands, neither is He served

by human hands as if He lacked anything—He, the
Giver of life and breath and all things to every one.
He has made from one person every nation of men
to settle on the entire surface of the earth . . . so that
they might seek for God, if only they would feel for
and find Him, although He is not far from each of
us; for 'in Him we live and move and have our being' (Ac 17:24-28, MLB*).

What is the apostle declaring? The old message
that "God is alive!"

He is alive and working in history, doing wonderful things! He created the universe and all it contains.
He is the Giver of life and breath and all things to
everyone. He made the human race to seek Him. Men
should feel for and find God who is not far away, but
as near as life, as close as the air we breathe.

This changeless passage stands as a rebuke to a
modern changing world. What a rebuke to the God-
is-dead theology and what a rebuke to the lifeless religious professions of our day! What a denial of materialism and atheism.

What a splendidly eloquent declaration that God
does meet people today!

And you are included!

The Book of Nature

God meets people in the Bible, of course. But even
if you're not partial to the Bible—God's book of re-

The Modern Language Bible: the New Berkeley Version in Modern English, rev. ed.

demption—He is still waiting to meet you in His book of nature.

In nature God reveals His wisdom and power to those willing to recognize Him.

Who has not been stopped in his tracks by a glorious sunrise or sunset? Who has failed to see how the firmament has been painted, with each fleecy cloud telling of the great artistry of the Creator. And when it is night, who can fail to see Him, in Longfellow's words, "in the infinite meadows of heaven (where) blossom the lovely stars, the forget-me-nots of the angels."

The psalmist, no mean poet either, pointed out that no language is needed to reveal God—not even a sound:

> The heavens are telling the glory of God,
>   and the firmament is showing His handiwork.
> Day after day pours forth speech,
>   and night after night declares knowledge.
>
> There is no speech, nor are there words;
>   their voice is not heard.
> Yet their line goes out through all the earth,
>   and their words to the end of the world.
>   (Ps 19:1-4, MLB)

If you miss God above as He reveals His glory in the heavens, perchance you will meet Him as He manifests Himself on the earth. See His majesty reflected in the towering redwoods of the California coast. Hear His voice in the wind singing through the pines or in the soft murmur of the brook meandering through the lea.

Remember that "from the creation of the world His invisible qualities, such as His eternal power and divine nature, have been made visible and have been understood through His handiwork" (Ro 1:20, MLB).

God is there in what we call "nature," by which we mean "God's wonderfully and gloriously created universe." He waits there to reveal Himself to you.

In a million wonders you can see the Creator manifested, with all His variety and wisdom, and the most cynical of atheists is not blind to the marvels of nature.

The animals are beautiful, powerful, and fearsome, but we men are not among them. We have souls to be awakened and we realize that we are not beasts. We are *man,* the highest of God's earthly creation, made to appreciate, know, and have fellowship with the Eternal.

Why, then, do men prefer to be like the beasts— blind to God's glory and beauty revealed in nature, and utterly unresponsive to the Creator? It is as if God peeks out of every nook and cranny, peering at the people—with some of the people pretending they do not see.

God beckons from every flower, every tree, every verdant meadow, every snowy, ice-bedecked forest. He winks (I say it worshipfully) in ten million darts of light as the sun kisses the waves of the sea. He displays His glory as a gentle breeze caresses the placid lake and scatters moonbeams in a stream of broken gold that for sheer beauty defies description.

He calls to men to take time to enjoy His creation.

And surely, to enjoy Him, the Creator.

The Book of Redemption

But if you do not easily read the book of nature, there still is, as I have said, the book of redemption.

Here, in a far more vital way—in an intimate way —God is waiting to meet you. This encounter will be yours if you read and receive the message of His great book of redemption.

It is popularly called the Bible, which means "The Book." This is appropriate. It is surely *the* book, par excellence. It is the Book of books, because it is a divine-human book, different from all the other books, which are purely human.

The Bible is really a love story. It is the greatest love story ever told. It is the story of God's love for the entire world—for each and every lost sinner among the billions.

It is the story of God's love for *you.*

And no other love story can approach its scope and wonder.

The Bible tells how God in the person of Jesus Christ, the eternal Word, came from heaven to earth to meet sinful man. God actually entered the human family and became a man—the God-man—God and man united in one glorious person.

The God-man, Jesus Christ, is literally the world's

Saviour. He died on the Cross of Calvary to redeem men—to pay for their sins and accept their penalty in their place. He rose from the dead and ascended to heaven from which He came. He sent the Holy Spirit to take His place and work in man the great salvation Christ purchased for humanity by His atoning death.

And that is the good news. That is the greatest love story ever told.

The story of the Saviour's atoning death is called "the Gospel," literally meaning "the good news." And the Gospel is not dead. The best news of all the good news is that *God is continuing to meet peope today!* He meets them in astonishing and miraculous ways— when men believe the good news that Jesus Christ, the God-man, died for their sins and rose again for their justification, *God saves them* the moment they believe.

What does that mean—*God saves them?* Well, it will take the rest of our lives here and the rest of eternity to fully appreciate that in all its wonder. But when God saves a man He forgives that man's sin and makes him, according to the book of redemption, a saint. He gives him a new heart and a new life—the very life of God in his soul. It is called eternal life because it will last forever, as long as God lasts.

This means that the man whom God saves is going to live forever with God. But while he lives in time—in this life—he will know and love God. He will be a member of God's family. God becomes his Father and he becomes a son in the divine family.

Does God meet people today? Yes, as always. Will

He meet you? Again, yes. Part of the good news is
for you. You play one of the leading roles in His love
story.

Believe that He loves you and that He gave Jesus
Christ to die for you.

Your meeting with God will be the supreme experience of your life!

3

WHO IS GOD?

In order to meet God we have to know who He is, what He is like and something about His provisions to meet *us*.

We have to know Him as He reveals Himself in His Word, not as He is defined by some sect or anti-sect of some religion, or some anti-religion.

Our human perspective is woefully limited in considering God, but we have the Scriptures to help us.

Know first that your meeting with God is no accident—at least not according to God. God's encounter with a man is never an afterthought but is always foreknown and preplanned by God in terms of eternity. God chose us in Christ "before the world was founded" and in love "predestined us in Jesus Christ to be His sons, in agreement with the kind intent of His will" (Eph 1:4-5, MLB).

He has already set up the terms for your meeting with Him, and it is essential that you understand them. Obviously, if you are going to meet God, you will have to meet Him as He is, not as you might make Him out to be in your own thinking.

Meeting a Bogus God

Millions of people never meet God because they have conjured up some other god.

Atheists believe in no god, of course, and that eliminates the true God along with all the phonies.

But there are millions who are not atheists. They profess to "believe in God," and yet they have never actually met Him. They believe in a god of their own fabrication. God is to them what they think He ought to be, rather than what He is and has said that He is. He becomes a product of their imaginations which has no real existence. He is the leading character of a multitude of spiritual fairy tales.

Donald Duck exists, insofar as he was created by the cartoonist Walt Disney, but we really don't expect to meet him by a pond some day. He is a product of fantasy. And we can as logically expect to meet Donald Duck or Snow White and the Seven Dwarfs on the street as we can expect to have a true spiritual encounter with a fabricated god.

The characters of fairy tales serve some human purposes. But they are not meant to be substitutes for the realities that should be known and experienced in our spiritual existence on earth.

People should not reasonably expect to encounter a god of their own manufacture who bears no resemblance to the God of the Bible—the God who met Abraham, Moses, Isaiah, Paul, Augustine, Luther, Wesley, and Whitefield. The God encountered by those worthies, at times when the pagans around them were fabricating an enormous variety of false gods, is the One available today.

His miraculous, life-changing characteristics are verifiably intact. And it is no more difficult to encounter Him now than at any time in the past.

The Most Popular Phony Gods

Some phony gods have done better than others in terms of their popularity. It is not that they bear more of the characteristics of the true God, but that they have been designed to more closely fulfill what unspiritual men think their needs are.

Consider the myriad gods of ancient paganism who engaged in endless bickerings and jealousies. Men fabricated such gods in order to relieve their own guilt feelings about such behavior. Those were gods they could "live with." They were no better than men, and thus men became as good as gods.

Today, the phony god concept has advanced, with the rest of worldly learning, so that the new phonies at least challenge the worldly imagination.

The most successful phony god is the one worshiped by atheists—the "non-existent god." He has a lot to offer. He doesn't require obedience, faith, prayer, or even recognition. (Of course, many atheists spend a lot of time and energy fighting the true God and His followers, so that, in a way, their non-god does require some effort.)

While the non-existent god requires nothing in the way of worship, he offers nothing in the way of reward. And, most pathetically, he causes men to pervert their natures. The commonsense witness of a man's brain, which sees the wonders of nature, the intricate mechanism of the physical universe, and the confounding complexity of other men, is subverted to the idea that there is no Creator. The magnificent human dignity available to those rightly related to God is given a colossal affront. The man, made in God's image, is relegated to slavery to other, more powerful men, and is denied the freedom of fellowship with God.

God is aware of this travesty. He refers, in His Word, to the man who says in his heart there is no God, and He terms him a "fool" (Ps 14:1).

Forced atheism hardly brings greater freedom, as is loudly claimed. One has to look only at Russia and China to see the atheistic brand of freedom in action.

Of course atheism to exist doesn't need a government or a big political system. Any man—and all men have been created with the right to a free choice—may be an atheist in his own right. But the result of choosing atheism is inevitable. Man simply becomes a slave to other men, and to whatever political, spiritual, or material system they may devise.

Deism is another kind of atheism which grants at least the former existence of God. The deist acknowledges that God created the universe, but holds that He withdrew from the management area, leaving the universe to sustain *itself*. Rejecting revealed religion, the information available about God through His Word and the revelations pertaining to it, the deist thinks that the universe is self-developing. He comes finally to the untenable concept that man himself is steadily improving.

Deism, because of its seriously incomplete and defective concept of God, unavoidably leads to atheism.

Pantheism sees the whole universe as God. Confusing the Creator with the creation, the pantheist's phony god is seen in everything around him—men, angels, good, evil. Virtually everything becomes a manifestation of God, including sin and all material things.

This thinking underlies much of oriental mysticism and ancient Greek philosophy and religion. According to the pantheistic line, man is a transient form of universal being no more immortal than the leaves of the forest or the waves of the sea. And actually, this is the most devastating form of atheism. Mere atheism is impartial—it deifies neither man nor evil. Man is not god, and nothing else is god, with "orthodox" atheists. But pantheism, in seeing God in everything, makes the human soul the highest form in which God exists, and evil is as much a manifestation of God as is good.

The agnostic takes a gutless position. He repudiates the possibility that God can be known, if he believes that God exists at all. He expresses his disbelief in terms of doubt unlike the atheist, who at least has conviction.

There are myriad other phony gods with varying degrees of acceptance and popularity, but the positions cited above serve our purposes in demonstrating dead-end streets. The point is, if a man is to experience an encounter with God, he must get rid of false notions about who God is, or whether He exists.

Concepts of God represented by atheism, deism, pantheism, and agnosticism are like fallen trees lying across the road blocking the way to the true God.

The True God

Theism is belief in God. It holds that a personal God exists as Creator, Preserver, Sustainer, and Ruler of all things. It draws its information about God from the Bible.

The idea that God is a Person, which is sharply opposed to the non-God concepts we discussed above, means simply that He possesses the attributes of personality. He has intellect, or the power of thinking (Pr 15:3; Jer 29:11; Heb 4:13), sensibility, or the power of feeling (Ps 33:5; 103:8-13; Ja 5:11) and volition, or the power of will (Ps 115:3; Dan 4:35; Mt 19:26).

Although God is a Person, Scripture reveals that His essence is "tri-personal," existing as Father, Son, and Holy Spirit. This description of God is doctrinally set forth under the term "Trinity," which evidently came into use in the second century A.D. Theophilus, Bishop of Antioch (168-183), was apparently the first Christian scholar to use that term.

The concept of the Trinity is thoroughly scriptural. It acknowledges both the unity of God (Ex 20:3-7; Deu 6:4-5) and the clear distinction of persons in the Godhead (Mt 28:19; Jn 14:16; 17:20-23; 2 Co 13:14). Deity is ascribed to each member of the

Trinity (Jn 1:1; Ac 5:3-4), along with mutual knowledge and love (Mt 11:27; 1 Co 2:10; Jn 3:35; Ro 8:27). To each member of the Trinity is assigned distinct but related offices (1 Co 12:4-6; Eph 2:18-22).

The orthodox formula of the doctrine of the Trinity held by sound biblical Christianity through the centuries is: "Three Persons in One Essence and One Essence manifested in Three Persons." Or, more simply, "Unity in Trinity and Trinity in unity."

Errors Concerning the Godhead

Scripture reveals much more about God than the Trinity, of course, but we bring it up here because it most manifestly contrasts the true God with the various false god concepts. Few of the myriad heresies about God comprehend the Trinity.

Nevertheless, even when the Trinity is recognized, mistakes are made (or concepts which manifestly disagree with Scripture).

Sabellianism, an early heresy, espoused a modal Trinity, clouding the personal distinctions in the true Trinity and seeing mere different manifestations of one Person. It persists today in certain Pentecostal sects.

Arianism preferred to see the Son as subordinate to the Father, rather than coequal. Arius, a presbyter of the church at Alexandria, Egypt, taught that the Son was not of the same essence as the Father, but was a creature, although the first and highest of all the creatures. He said, "If the son were truly a son, there must have been a time when he was not (did not exist)."

The council of Nicaea condemned Arianism in A.D. 325, but its concept of deity existing only in one person has come down to us as Unitarianism. Variant forms of Arianism prevail today in the Mormons, Jehovah's Witnesses, and other sects that deny the Trinity and the full deity of Christ.

Swedenborgianism and Tritheism, which holds to three Gods, also violate the scriptural concept of the Trinity.

We Must Understand Christ

The common problem about the Trinity shared by all these heretical concepts is that they fail to give the Saviour His due. He is certainly not superior to the other members of the Trinity, but where men are concerned it is He who brings salvation. "I am the way, the truth and the life," He advises us. A failure to recognize His mission undermines the wonderful story of redemption in the Bible.

If Christ is "the way," and if we are to meet with the Father, then we must see Christ in His own Person. The Son put it emphatically: "no man comes to the Father, but through me" (Jn 14:6). We must enquire, "Who is He? Who was He before He became a man? Who was He after He assumed humanity? Did He, in fact, die and then rise from death? Who and where is He *now?*"

The only reliable description of Jesus is in the Scripture, of course, though many thinkers, theological, philosophical, and literary, have rendered opinions about Him. Scripture gives a full and satisfying picture of our Saviour, and why shouldn't it, after all? The Bible is, in essence, the story of redemption, and Jesus is the Redeemer and the central character of that story.

In that all the plans and purposes of God for time and eternity point obviously toward redemption it would be strange if revealed truth failed to give a clear presentation of the Saviour and His work.

Who Was Christ Before His Birth?

Jesus declared that He was the one and only way to God, and that he who had seen Him had seen the Father (Jn 14:9). What sort of person was He that He could make such statements?

Unless those declarations were no more than colossal pride and blasphemy, Jesus was the most unique and unusual Person who ever lived. He was in fact saying that He was God!

And truly, the Scriptures urge upon us that He *was* God. He was the eternal Word who was "with God and was God," and thus He existed from all eternity. He eternally resided in the bosom of the Father (Jn 1:18) and He possessed the divine attributes of eternity (Mic 5:2), immutability (Heb 1:11-12; 13:8), omnipotence (1 Co 15:28; Phil 3:21), omniscience (Rev 1:8), and omnipresence (Mt 28:20).

As God, Christ manifested His deity in His mighty

works of creation, preservation, forgiveness of sin, and the miracles of His resurrection and ascension to heaven.

He was the Creator of the universe: "All things were made by him; and without him was not any thing made that was made" (Jn 1:3, KJV). In His deity as "the image of the invisible God," He is described as "the firstborn of all creation" (Col 1:15). "For by him were all things created ... all things were created by him, and for him" (Col 1:16, KJV) and, plainly, "He is before all things" (Col 1:17).

While Christ is typically referred to in the worldly religions as "a great moral teacher" (if that!) we can see from the Word that He is surely infinitely more.

As the Creator, Christ holds together what He put together when He made the universe: "In Him all things hold together" (Col 1:17). He made the atom by His creative power, and by the same power He holds it together. Thus, the universe continues to function.

When He finally removes His almighty hand, prophecy intimates, the atom will dissolve and the resulting heat will purge the earth, preparing the way for the new heaven and new earth in which righteousness will dwell (2 Pe 3:7-12; Rev 21:1).

It obviously pays to know Christ. If we are to dwell in that kingdom to come, where God's will will be done on earth as it is in heaven, we must know our Saviour completely. A look at His life and His mission is not only expedient but deeply inspiring.

Read on.

4

THE SIN-AND-DEATH-CONQUERING CHRIST

We have seen that Scripture describes plainly the eternal nature of Christ (Jn 1:2; Phil 2:5-11; Heb 1:1-3). Interestingly, many passages discuss or imply His activity before His earthly birth.

In prayer to His Father the Saviour said, "And now, O Father, glorify thou me with thine own self with the glory which I had with thee before the world was" (Jn 17:5, KJV) The apostle Paul taught that Christ existed "in the form of God" before He humbled Himself to become a man (Phil 2:6).

In Old Testament times Christ appeared as the Angel of Jehovah. As the Messenger of the covenant He revealed Himself to Abraham, Hagar, Isaac, Jacob, and Moses. He led Israel out of Egypt. He administered the Law at Sinai. He showed Himself to Gideon (Judg 6:22-24) and the parents of Samson (Judg 13:20-23). He was seen by Joshua (Josh 5:13-15), Isaiah (Is 6:1-5) and many of the other Old Testament saints.

He enraged His audience (Jn 8:58) with the momentous statement, "Before Abraham was, I am."

God Becomes Man

The resplendent central truth of Christianity is that Christ, the eternally existing Creator of the universe, very God of very God, in the course of time chose to become a man. The Word, who was with God and was God, took upon Himself humanity.

The Creator united with the creature and entered the human family.

This marvel of marvels was made possible by the virgin birth (Mt 1:18-25). The Holy Spirit generated the sinless humanity of Christ in the womb of Mary of Nazareth (Lk 1:35). Thus, the eternal Word, the preincarnate Christ, united Himself to that sinless humanity to form the God-man Jesus Christ. In this way God identified Himself with the human race. The second person of the Trinity joined Himself to mankind. The divine nature and the human nature were merged and the two natures became the glorious divine-human person of Jesus Christ incarnate.

Obviously, if this scriptural account of the conception and birth of Jesus Christ is true, our Lord is absolutely different from every other human being. Because He represented the union of two natures, He is set forth in the Scriptures under various "son-titles" that define His roles.

Christ's title *Son of God* presents Him in His deity. *Son of Man* indicates His humanity. *Son of Mary* shows Him to be a born member of the human race. *Son of David* connects Him with His Jewish ancestry and Messianic mission. *Son of Abraham* identifies Him as the promised Redeemer of mankind.

His complete and official title is the Lord Jesus
Christ (2 Th 1:1; Gal 1:1). The title Lord, connec-
ting with Jehovah of the Old Testament, indicates His
deity. The human name Jesus, meaning literally redeemer or savior, points to His mission as Saviour
through His sacrifice (Mt 1:2). The title Christ,
meaning the anointed one, relates Him to all that is
foretold of the Messiah in the Old Testament as
prophet, priest, and king. Thus the designation "Lord
Jesus Christ" sums up the exalted character and
work of the one who bears this name. Indeed, it is as
elevated as the term "God" with which it is equated.

The deity of God the Son appears in the fact that
divine attributes are ascribed to Him. He is, first of
all, declared to be eternal (Is 9:6; Mic 5:2; Jn 1:1-
2). His title "Father of Eternity" actually means in
Hebrew idiom, "The Eternally Existing One" (Is
9:6). He is immutable (Ps 102:25-27; Heb 1:10-
12; 13:8), omnipotent (Rev 1:8; Phil 3:21), omniscient (Jn 10:15; 21:17), and omnipresent (Mt
18:20, 28:20). He is life itself, and the source of all
life, physical, spiritual, and eternal (Jn 1:4; 14:6).
He is truth itself and the source of all truth (Jn 14:6;
Rev 3:7). He is infinitely holy (Lk 1:35; Jn 6:69;
Heb 7:26). He is *love,* and this attribute is the essence of His Being (Jn 13:1, 34; 1 Jn 3:16).

Divine prerogatives are assigned to Christ as God.
He is the Creator of all things (Jn 1:3; Col 1:16).
He is Preserver of all things (Col 1:17). He forgives
sin (Lk 5:24; Col 3:3). He will raise the dead (Jn

5:28-29). He will reward the saints (2 Co 5:10). To Him is committed all judgment (Jn 5:22).

And He is worshiped as God (Jn 5:23; Lk 24:52).

When we contemplate the wonder that One who was God freely chose to become mere man, with all the trouble and agony that it entailed, we cannot help but be impressed with the extent of Christ's sacrifice. We shall receive the free gift of salvation, paid for by the Anointed One, in humble worship and adoration.

The Life of Christ

The earthly life of Jesus Christ has confounded secular and theological historians and scholars since the first century. Believers and non-believers alike are mystified by the perfection of a man who was apparently a humble carpenter of Galilee. A life lived in sinlessness, compassion, and humility was and is beyond the ken of any living man. A life such as that lived by Jesus of Nazareth is beyond the boundaries of human experience.

Many a non-believer, even many an atheist, has had to admit, perhaps grudgingly, that Jesus Christ in His ministry to little Israel was the most startling feature of human history.

Besides the marvel of His perfectly lived life is the fact that it is efficacious toward men. His redemptive work—His sacrifice on the cross—freed all men from their endless bondage to sin. Free for the taking, His sacrifice eternally affects each and every human being.

He could do for men what He did on the cross because of who He was from all eternity. He, the infinite, unlimited God, came out of the corridors of timelessness to limit Himself to the confines of a tiny babe fashioned in a virgin's womb. He chose to circumscribe his glorious deity within the bounds of the finite body of an ordinary man.

The apostle Paul describes this mysterious and awesome self-editing of deity. "Though existing in the form of God," Christ "did not consider His equality with God something to cling to, but emptied Himself as He took on the form of a slave and became like human beings. So, recognized in appearance as a human being, He humbled Himself and became obedient to death; yes, death by the cross" (Phil 2:6-8, MLB).

One of the major events in the earthly life of the God-man Redeemer was His baptism by John in the Jordan River. As the heavens opened and the Spirit of God descended upon Him on that occasion, He was consecrated to His great messianic ministry of Prophet, Priest, and King.

The voice of the Father in Heaven gave the divine approbation, "This is My Son, the Beloved in whom I delight" (Mt 3:17, MLB).

As Prophet, Christ gave far-reaching information concerning the messianic kingdom, the coming age of the Church, the tribulation, His second advent, the millennium, and the eternal state. As Priest, our Lord was set apart for His redemptive ministry and offered Himself as the sacrifice (Heb 7:27), purchasing eternal salvation for all who believe (Heb 9:12). As

King, He was rejected at His first advent, but will reign as absolute ruler at His second advent, to restore the kingdom to Israel (Ac 1:6; Rev 19:16).

Another important epoch in the earthly life of Christ was His temptation (Mt 4:1; Mk 1:2-13; Lk 4:1-13). It was the crucial attack of Satan against His humanity. The issue at stake was whether or not He would abide in His Father's will when presented with the seductions of the enemy. At stake as well, of course, was the salvation of all mankind.

That Christ would resist Satan and carry on in His mission was assured by His very nature as God, and was determined from all eternity. Yet the test was allowed so that finite minds might be assured of the sinlessness of the Redeemer.

Another mountain-peak experience in the earthly life of the incarnate Son was "the transfiguration." This remarkable event presented a graphic picture of the glory of the future kingdom (Mt 16:28; Mk 9:1; Lk 9:27). It signaled a new development in the career of the Messiah. Up to this point, He had devoted Himself to the kingdom ministry which had engaged John the Baptist and the disciples. Now the divine purpose to call out the Church was announced (Mt 16: 21-23). This would be accomplished, of course, through the death and resurrection of the Messiah.

Thus, the Messiah came and preached the kingdom to men. They did not receive His teachings, nor Him for that matter. For this reason Israel was temporarily set aside, and the Church age was ushered in. The Messiah had to go to a cruel earthly death and be resurrected to consummate the divine redemptive program.

This new turn of events necessitated that the kingdom not only be promised but actually displayed. The transfiguration gave an unforgettable example to those who saw and reported it. The future of the kingdom was thus guaranteed, and the disappointment occasioned by the rejection and impending death of the King was not allowed to crush out the hope of the eventual establishment of His reign on the earth.

No consideration of the earthly life of Christ would be complete without touching upon His remarkable teachings—what He said. Even His enemies had to admit, "Never did a man speak the way this man speaks!" (Jn 7:46). As He ministered in the synagogue at Nazareth, all the people wondered "at the gracious words which were falling from His lips" (Lk 4:22).

The words of Christ, as recorded in the Gospels, especially those contained in His major discourses, present clearly the purpose and scope of His advent both to His own nation, Israel, and to the Church. They are models of clear thinking, inspiration, and unheard-of perceptions of things.

Debate with the most adept legal minds of Israel and the hostile priesthood presented no difficulty to the carpenter of Galilee. The learned Nicodemus was astonished by the plainspoken pronouncements of the Teacher who understood the hidden meaning of life, death, and the universe.

The saved and the lost alike are continually shaken

by the mind of Christ, as expressed in the lessons He taught in the cities and on the mountains of the Holy Land.

Ranking in wonder with what Christ said in the course of His earthly ministry is what He did. He performed many mighty works. These signs and miracles were done, of course, to relieve human misery. But they also had a far wider purpose in attesting our Lord's claim to be the Messiah and the Saviour of the world. People who saw His miracles, however, still withheld their faith in many cases. The Messiah sadly declared, "Had I not accomplished the works among them which no other ever accomplished, they would not be guilty; but now they have seen and have hated both Me and My Father" (Jn 15:24, MLB).

Who He was, together with what He did and said in His tabernacling in human flesh, combine to make His life incomparable and unique. Although He came to save sinners and freely mingled with them, He Himself was sinless. He was attested to be "holy, harmless, undefiled, separate from sinners" (Heb 7:26, KJV). "In all points tempted like as we are" (Heb 4:15 KJV), He was not only "without sin" but was filled with divine love and every resplendent virtue in a degree which is to us immeasurable. The Christian poet Thomas O. Chisholm commemorated His life:

> Behold One cometh in the way,
>   In humble garments clad;
> The poorest of the poor is He,
>   No pillow for His head.

The hungry, weary, sick and sad
   In crowds around Him press,—
To everyone He gives relief,—
   "What manner of man is this?"

What words of grace and truth He speaks,
   Ne'er heard on earth before:
The burdened sinner hears that voice,
   And feels his sins no more;
He calls the dead to life again,
   Bids winds and billows cease,
None other man such works hath done,—
   "What manner of man is this?"

The Death of Christ

The crucifixion of the carpenter of Nazareth would be, of course, the saddest of events, were it not for its profound implications for all of mankind. With His life being so transcendently wonderful, we could reasonably expect His death to be glorious as well.

Behind the bloody sweat and anguish of Gethsemane, behind the awful darkness and death of Calvary, shines forth the splendor of God's gracious love for sinners. This mystic glow has illumined the centuries with its wondrous warmth. It has lightened the hearts of millions of sinners throughout the ages who have reposed their faith in the Saviour. As the purest lily grows out of the rankest mire, so the holy love of God springs forth from the dark, dismal expression of man's wickedness perpetrated on Golgotha.

Who can fathom the terrible cry from the cross,

"My God, My God, why hast Thou forsaken me?"
(Ps 22:1; Mt 27:46) as the Father turned His face
away from the Son. Who can comprehend the as-
tounding fact that the One "who knew no sin," God
"made sin on our behalf, so that in Him we might
share the righteousness of God" (2 Co 5:21, MLB)?

But from the fall of man and the first enunciation
of the Gospel of grace (Gen 3:15, 21), God required
that animal sacrifices be killed and the blood sprink-
led. Our Saviour willingly submitted to death, even
the grossly ignominious "death on a cross" (Phil 2:8).

> From Calvary a cry was heard—
>   A bitter and heart-rending cry;
> My Saviour! ev'ry mournful word
>   Bespoke Thy soul's deep agony.
>
> A horror of great darkness fell
>   On Thee, Thou spotless, holy One!
> And all the eager hosts of hell
>   Conspired to tempt God's only Son.
>
> The scourge, the thorns, the deep disgrace—
>   These thou coulds't bear, nor once repine;
> But when Jehovah veiled His face,
>   Unutterable pangs were Thine.
>
> Let the dumb world its silence break;
>   Let pealing anthems rend the sky;
> Awake my sluggish soul wake!
>   He died, that we might never die.
>   JOHN W. CUNNINGHAM

What Christ Accomplished at Calvary

Calvary was a dark scene indeed. So dark there was midnight gloom at midday (Mt 27:45). But out of that darkness has burst forth light. Calvary's gleam has girdled the globe. While it reveals the abysmal sin of the human heart, at the same time it publishes the Gospel of God's love that rescues man from sin and floods his soul with salvation.

It is difficult to describe all that Calvary accomplished for it accomplished so much. First and foremost, Christ's death as a substitute sacrifice set free God's gracious love to act on behalf of fallen humanity without compromising His infinite holiness.

Calvary in other words establishes God as righteous and holy. As a result of Christ's death God could forgive the sins that in Old Testament times had been covered temporarily by animal sacrifices as a debt is covered by a promissory note. In Christ God has bought up all the promissory notes. His full payment for sin in Christ's death shows that He was right in not judging man immediately back then. Even now God's full payment for sin by Christ establishes God as right when He freely forgives the sinner who does nothing but trust in Christ as his Substitute and Saviour.

In enabling God to save sinners, the death of Christ accomplished what the Scriptures call a "propitiation" or satisfaction (Ro 3:25; 1 Jn 2:2; 4:10). God was satisfied regarding the debt that man owed Him because of sin's guilt. Now God is morally free to exercise His grace and love in fully forgiving all those who trust in the Saviour.

In rendering the fallen race savable, the death of Christ accomplished what the Bible calls a "reconciliation." "God was in Christ reconciling the world to Himself, not counting their trespasses against them" (2 Co 5:19). Through Christ's death the position of the world was *completely changed* from a state of hopeless lostness to "savableness." Man was, in effect, salvaged.

Formerly the world was without hope of salvaging. Sin had alienated man from God, separating him from life and fellowship with God. Now the cross provides the basis for a new hope. The world can be saved (1 Co 5:19).

"Therefore, we are ambassadors for Christ, as though God were entreating through us; we beg you on behalf of Christ, be reconciled to God" (1 Co 5:20). "For if while we were enemies, we were reconciled to God through the death of His Son, much more, having been reconciled, we shall be saved by His life. And not only this, but we also exult in God through our Lord Jesus Christ, through whom we have now received the reconciliation (Ro 5:10-11).

Besides propitiation toward God and reconciliation toward man, Christ's death effected redemption toward sin. All of Adam's fallen race are slaves, sold into bondage to sin (Ro 7:14) and are helplessly condemned to death (Jn 3:18; Gal 3:10). Christ, as the sinner's Substitute, paid the ransom price of death (Heb 9:27-28). Spiritually redeemed, the emancipated sinner never returns to his former condition of slavery, but is set free forever (Jn 8:36; Ro 8:19-21).

Christ's death also was a grand demonstration that lost sinners of Adam's fallen race can never be saved by a legal system of meritorious works, but solely by the grace of God through faith on the part of the sinner (Eph 2:8-10). No one is able to "earn" salvation.

After Adam fell, man's only possible approach to God was through the shedding of blood in animal sacrifice (Gen 3:15, 21; 4:4; 8:20; 12:8; etc.). The Mosaic system of works given to the nation Israel pointed to the same fact (Gal 3:19-25). Christ's death brought the Gospel of grace into clearest focus. His blood was shed as our approach to God.

When Christ died, the entire race of sinners was presented with the good news that His sacrifice secured the righteous ground upon which God can justify sinners without compromising His infinite holiness. He imputes His own righteousness to believing sinners. He sees them in the perfections of His own Son. He receives them *totally* apart from anything they are in themselves or do in themselves. They are *wholly* accepted in what they are in Christ and what Christ has done for them.

There is another marvelous thing our Saviour accomplished at Calvary. His death solved not only the problem of personal sins. It solved the problem of the "sin nature" as well. As our Substitute, Christ "died for our sins" (1 Co 15:3). He also "died to sin" (Ro 6:10). The latter point declares that He brought the very sin nature into judgment. "He condemned sin in the flesh" (Ro 8:3). This does not mean the old nature is destroyed nor that its essential power is diminished. It does mean, however, that God had in view the provision of a righteous basis upon which the old nature may be wholly controlled by the Spirit of God.

What a relief! Despite the fact that as a redeemed man I still possess the old nature, which I had as a sinner, I now also possess a new nature and the indwelling Spirit. As a result I can live triumphantly over sin! Why? Because Christ judged the old nature when He died. Now the Holy Spirit not only resides in my body as a holy temple, but He can make my body an instrument of holy living and serving. And most wonderful of all—God's own infinite holiness is not compromised.

The same glorious fact appears in the problem of the believer's forgiveness and cleansing when he sins (1 Jn 1:7-9). This cleansing is accomplished on the basis of what the Christian is in Christ, and what Christ has done for him on the cross. A once-for-all cleansing is part of the saving grace of God toward all who believe and are saved (Jn 13:10). This includes sins contracted in a Christian's daily walk.

Sins break fellowship with God. If fellowship is to be restored, the believer must "confess" his sins. He must honestly face them and forsake them, knowing they are forgiven by the efficacy of Christ's blood (1 Jn 1:7), attested by Christ's heavenly advocacy (1 Jn 2: 1-2). When confession is made, communion with the Father and Son is restored. But it must always be remembered, (and is all too often forgotten) that the believer's salvation is never for one moment the issue. The issue is wholly the believer's *fellowship* with God, not His *position* before God. Salvation cannot be forfeited.

Many more wonderful things were accomplished by our Lord when He died on Calvary. Volumes have been written on this inexhaustible theme. A few of the more glorious and far-reaching results have been mentioned. It will take eternity to discover all that was wrought there when the incarnate Creator-Redeemer bowed His head in death and cried, "It is finished!" (Jn 19:30).

> Hark! the voice of love and mercy
> 　　Sounds aloud from Calvary;
> See, it rends the rocks asunder
> 　　Shakes the earth and veils the sky:
>
> "It is finished! It is finished!"
> 　　Hear the dying Saviour cry!
>
> It is finished—oh, what pleasure
> 　　Do those precious words afford!
> Heavenly blessings, without measure,
> 　　Flow to us from Christ, the Lord.
> "It is finished! It is finished!"
> 　　Saints the dying words record.
> 　　　　　　　　　BENJAMIN FRANCIS

Rejoicing in Christ's Resurrection

The great central truth of the Gospel is that Christ died, was buried, and rose again from the dead (1 Co 15:3-4). Apart from these events there is no Gospel. Our Saviour's burial attested His death. As the type of the Scapegoat, which carried away Israel's guilt into the wilderness on the great day of national atonement (Lev 16:10), Christ bore away the burden of sin into oblivion. His lifeless body was placed in Joseph's new tomb, carved from the solid rock. There He lay as the sin-bearer of the fallen race.

But from death He came forth in glorious resurrection as the Lord of glory, Head of the new creation.

Next to the nativity, the resurrection of Christ is the most joyous celebration of the Christian calendar. Christmas with its message of the Christ Child cradled in the manger in Bethlehem and its angelic chorus appearing to humble shepherds on the Judean hills is indeed most solemnly wonderful. But Easter, commemorating the empty tomb and the death-conquering Christ, is a climactic event that gives meaning to all the events in our Lord's earthly career that preceded it.

The central importance of the resurrection is everywhere emphasized in the Scriptures. Christ came forth from the grave in a glorified deathless human body because of Who He was—God and man in one person. "Him God raised up by setting Him free from the pangs of death; for He could not be held in its

grip" (Ac 2:24, MLB). It was impossible that the
eternal Word made flesh could be bound by death.

"According to the Spirit of holiness" Christ "was
openly designated as the Son of God with power when
He was raised from the dead" (Ro 1:3-4, MLB). The
resurrection attested His glorious Person and the absolute efficacy of His redemptive work (Ro 4:25). It
established Christ's headship over the Church, His
Body (Eph 1:22-23). It constituted Him the Be-
stower of resurrection life to all who believe on Him
(Jn 12:24).

Christ came forth from death in resplendent glory
to be the "first-fruits," and the example of all who
will be glorified in Him (1 Co 15:20-23; Phil 3:20-
21). He stepped forth from the empty tomb in His
glorified humanity to rise to an exalted position at the
right hand of God waiting for that day when He returns to reign on earth. Then He will sit on David's
throne ruling Israel and the entire world. Then He
will fulfill all the covenants and promises made to
Israel under the old economy (Ac 2:30).

So important in the sight of God is the resurrection
of Christ that it is to be commemorated once every
week. In honor of this stupendous event the first day
of the week is set aside in the present age to celebrate
the new creation in Christ and supplants the Sabbath
of the old order.

Christ's Ascension and Present Ministry

The sequel to the resurrection of Christ was His
departure for heaven to take up His present ministry

there. Two "ascensions" are set forth in Scripture. One occurred immediately after Christ came forth from the tomb. The glorified Christ returned to heaven as the firstfruits of those resurrected, and as Priest presenting His blood as the token of His completed redemption (Jn 20:17). The other ascension after He was seen by the Disciples and others, marked Christ's final departure from the earth to undertake His present ministry in heaven (Lk 27:50).

Upon His arrival in heaven Christ sent the Holy Spirit to take His place upon earth (Jn 14:16-18) and to effect the salvation purchased at Calvary in those who would believe (Ac 2:38-41). The earthly ministry of the Spirit in effecting Christ's salvation in believers became coupled with the heavenly ministry of Christ's high-priestly intercession. The latter guarantees the eternity and unforfeitability of that glorious salvation.

In His present intercessory work our great heavenly High Priest takes into account the weakness and immaturity of His own who are in the world (Ro 8:34; Heb 7:25). As our Advocate, He defends His own before the Father's throne when they sin (Ro 8:34; Heb 9:24; 1 Jn 2:1). His defense is based on the complete efficacy of His finished redemptive work and the justification for time and eternity of all who are saved and united to Him.

How wonderfully reassuring to consider the greatness of the salvation Christ has purchased, and the safety and security of it guaranteed by His present ministry in our behalf at the right hand of the Father!

It is exhilarating to recognize also that in His present work our Lord exercises universal authority, with "all power" given to Him "in heaven and on earth" (Mt 28:18). As Head of all matters that pertain to the Church (Eph 1:22-23), He bestows and directs the exercise of spiritual gifts in the body of Christ (Ro 12:3-8; 1 Co 12: 4-31; Eph 4:7-11).

It is marvelous also to realize that our Lord, in His exalted position, is building the place to which He has gone to prepare for His own to be our habitation for eternity (Jn 14:1-3). Meanwhile, as He sits with the Father on His Father's throne (Rev 3:21), He is "expecting" and awaiting that glorious hour when the kingdoms of this world shall become His kingdom, and He shall reign as absolute Lord on His own throne (Ps 103:1; Rev 19:16).

The Second Coming and the Kingdom

He is coming again in glory as a conquering King. His glorified saints will come with Him. He will strike death to His foes and take possession of the earth as absolute King and Lord (Rev 19:11-16). Satan and demon powers will be remanded to the abyss (Rev 20:1-3; cf. Zec 13:2). The earthly Davidic kingdom offered to Israel and rejected at His first advent will be set up at the second advent.

The Messiah's kingdom over Israel will extend to the nations of the world. Through it Christ will fulfill the expectations of the covenants and promises made in the Old Testament (Rev 20:4-10). His thousand-year mediatorial reign will constitute the last of the ordered ages of time.

Its end will mark the advent of eternity.

Christ's Eternal Reign

The end of the millennial kingdom and the dawn of the eternal state will witness the last revolt of Satan and sinners (Rev 20:7-10) and the final judgment of the wicked (Rev 20:11-15). In eternity all sin and sinners will be confined to gehenna, the lake of fire (Rev 20:11-15).

Eternity will embrace a new heaven, a new earth, a New Jerusalem and a sin-cleansed universe (Rev 21:1—22:5). Never will this blissful state be threatened by sin or sinners.

Christ will subdue all powers and the entire earth. Then He will officially submit all His kingdom to God as a trophy. God will receive His Son's gift and then allow Him to reign forever on David's throne as the God-man, the Ruler of God's kingdom on earth (2 Sa 2:16; Is 9:6-7; Lk 1:31-33; Rev 11:15).

Hallelujah! What a God and Saviour! He stands ready to meet us—poor sinners that we are! But if we are going to meet Him, we must face up to Him as Almighty God infinitely holy and loving, reaching out through Jesus Christ to draw us to Himself and enfold us in His forgiving love.

5

WHO ARE YOU?

So the stage has been completely set for the God-man encounter.

Salvation—the free gift of God through the sacrifice of the Saviour—is there for the asking; and God is ready to meet people today, as we have seen.

The next, consideration is *you*.

You have not merely to face up to God, but to yourself as well. If you are to meet God, you will have to see yourself as you really are and not as you imagine yourself to be. Just as it is necessary for you to see God as He really is, so you must see yourself as you really are.

The philosopher Rene Descartes challenged his students with the maxim Know Thyself. He was hitting a nerve; it is utterly amazing how few people really know themselves. People know their relatives and friends far better than they know themselves. Hence, they are much more critical of others and their faults than they are of themselves.

Ignorance of self is especially acute and disastrous in the spiritual realm. There the issue of God's evaluation of us comes into play. Of course, many people haven't bothered to contemplate what God thinks of them and, in fact, they couldn't care less. As a result self-deception is rampant and constitutes one of the chief barriers in the matter of meeting God.

To Begin—You Are God's Creation

The concept of man as merely an advanced animal is at odds with Scripture. The idea that man evolved from lower forms of life has received a lot of credence as a logical and even satisfying theory to those locked into material concepts of things. But theory is theory, not fact.

The origin of the species is clearly described in Scripture. To subscribe to unproved theory is to start out on a dead-end road that will never lead to God.

The evolutionary view of the origin of man actually dishonors God and degrades man. It is flatly contradicted by the Word of God. The Scriptures clearly teach that man was created by God (Gen 1:27; 2:7). The creation of man is presented as a direct act of God, completely distinct from His creation of the animal kingdom. God created man with a body, soul, and spirit, according to Scripture.

Thus, man as constituted by creation has both a material and an immaterial nature. The material nature is his body. The immaterial nature consists of his soul and spirit (Num 16:22; 1 Ki 17:21; 1 Co 2:11; Ja 2:26).

The soul is the principle of animal life. The spirit is the principal of rational, spiritual, and immortal being. At death the body dissolves into the dust from which it was made. The soul and the spirit, Scripture indicates, go to the spirit world. In the case of the believer, the destination is heaven, there to await the first resurrection and reunion with a glorified body outfitted for eternal fellowship with God.

In the case of the unbeliever, the destination is hades, there to await the second resurrection and reunion with a body fit only for eternal separation from God.

God's preference in this important matter is made clear. It is evident from Scripture that man was created by God for eternal fellowship with his Creator. But in His divine and eternal purpose God has allowed man, as well as all created intelligences, a choice in the matter. Man and angels who will enjoy eternal fellowship with their Creator will do so as free moral agents, who have made a free choice.

beatly. This fundamental difference between the high-

The same is true of those who choose the other option.

What Is Man?

Man is a moral creature. He didn't spring from animals to act like an animal. He is not an evolved beast who slips back on occasion to the jungle to act beastly. This fundamental difference between the highest of the animals and mankind is an unbridgable gap confounding evolution.

As a creature of God, man has a moral nature and is held morally responsible by his Creator.

Today evolution is being taught almost universally in our educational systems as if it were fact. And it leads to reasoning which runs approximately like this: If, after all, we are merely "super animals," not held morally responsible by a creator, then obviously we are free to create our own rules or abide by no rules at all. Actually, the latter is coming into fashion.

The moral responsibility of man to God is being set aside by today's new theologies and their concomitant loose morality. The results are ghastly. Set loose from God, man's greed, rebellion against all authority, and sexual license are threatening the very foundations of human life.

The Bible distinctly teaches that man is endowed with powers which equip him to distinguish between right and wrong actions. These powers include intellect, sensibility, will, conscience, and free moral agency. Intellect or the capacity of reason enables man to discern the difference between right and wrong. Sensibility gives him the capacity to be moved emotionally and responsibly. Free agency sets him at liberty to choose one course or the other.

"But in connection with these faculties there is a sort of activity which involves them all, and without which there can be no moral action namely, the activity of conscience. Conscience applies the moral law to particular cases in our personal experience, and proclaims that law is binding upon us. Only a rational and sentient being can be truly moral."[1]

"The voice of conscience, when normal to any degree, is ever true to the divine ideal."[2] The conscience operates despite the fact that there is much in fallen man which is contrary to God. Some regard conscience as not an integral part of man, but the voice of God acting as an inner monitor. However, this voice can be silenced only by persistent wrongdoing. Persistent wrongdoing will pervert and at last silence the voice of conscience.

There was once an Indian who bought a package of tobacco at a trading post and found a silver coin in it. His conscience was troubled. He came back and wished to return the coin. The trader laughed at his scruples.

But the Indian insisted. "I got a good man and a bad man in my heart," he said. "The good man say, 'It is not yours.' The bad man say, 'Nobody will know.' The good man say, 'Take it back.' The bad man say, 'Never mind.' So I think I go to sleep. But the good man and bad man talk all night and trouble me!"[3]

We experience the feeling of conflict when the conscience is in operating order and we have acted in a way that troubles it. Conscience, in working order, allows a man to make responsible and personal choices with respect to character and conduct. It clearly demonstrates him to be a moral creature. But when conscience is seared and branded into insensitivity by persistent wrongdoing (1 Ti 4:2), man sinks to the level of the brute, who has no conscience.

In these last days when lawlessness and occultism abound (2 Ti 3:1-13), and the inspiration and authority of God's Word are being flouted (2 Ti 3:14-17), we are seeing human beings behave with conscience inoperative.

Man Was Made in the Divine Image

Scripture distinctly teaches that man was created in the image and likeness of God (Gen 1:26; 5:1; 1 Co 11:7; Col 3:10). The divine image is reflected in man in a twofold way. It is seen in a natural likeness, or personality, and a moral likeness, or holiness.

Personality is that element of the divine image which makes a man a man and not an animal.

Ancient peoples like the Greeks recognized the dignity and God-likeness of personality, but they mistook it for divinity itself, rather than the divine image in reflection. They were unable to conceive that any object or force of nature could have life or beauty apart from it.

All the objects of the natural world were for them the expression of a person—a god, demi-god, dryad, grace, or nymph. For them, nature was alive and vibrant with personality—every tree, every flower, every waterfall, every star. Every bit and piece of their world had "personality."

But God's revelation confines personality to God's highest creature, man. By virtue of personality, with its constituent elements of intellect, sensibility, volition, self-consciousness, conscience, and moral choice, man at his creation was equipped to make intelligent choice. He could choose which element of his knowledge, whether God, self, or the world, would be the center of his development.

Man's likeness to God, as reflected in his personality, is inalienable. It cannot be lost. Man could not lose his personality without ceasing to be a man. Insanity, as terrible as it is, can only obscure it. Even eternal hell will not be able to obliterate it. It will remain indelible upon man as the token that he is the highest earthly creature of God, created directly by Him and not evolved. And since it contains a capacity for redemption, personality gives high value to the life even of the unregenerate (Gen 9:6; 1 Co 11:7; Ja 3:9).

For this reason human nature is to be reverenced. He who destroys human life is to be put to death (Gen 9:6), a divine law being widely set aside today in the general apostasy from God's Word.

The divine image is stamped upon man, secondly, in moral likeness or holiness. Scripture reveals that man was created pure and holy (Eph 4:24; Col 3:10). But unlike personality or natural likeness to God, which is unforfeitable, moral purity or holiness is forfeitable. It could be lost. And it was indeed lost by the original sin (Eph 4:23-24; Col 3:10).

Adam was created with a holy nature and imbued with tendencies toward God. But since the Fall, men are born with a sinful nature with tendencies away from God.

By creation man had a holy nature but not a holy character. The latter could only develop as man exercised his power of free choice in the presence of good and evil. This holy nature was more than innocence; it was a positive similarity to God in purity and rectitude.

Man's original moral likeness to God was to be

handed down to Adam's descendants, if retained. But even if it were lost to him and to them, in the event Adam sinned, it would still leave man his personality, his natural likeness to God, which left him susceptible to God's redeeming grace and hence saveable.

We have to fall back to the alternative, as things happened.

A High Purpose

Because he was created in the divine image and likeness, man's physical form apparently reflects an original heavenly type (Eze 1:26). The angelic beings (pure spirits) evidently have this form when visible, as did the preincarnate Christ, the Angel of the Lord.

Man's sensuous impulses were in subjection to the spirit. Man had dominion over the lower creation (Gen 1:26-28; Ps 8:5-8). He also enjoyed communion with God (Gen 3:8-9).

It seems that God manifested Himself to unfallen man in visible, perhaps angelic form (Gen 3:8). This spirit form bore a resemblance to man's material form. This fellowship was suited to man in his state of unconfirmed holiness (i.e., his holiness was subject to testing).

But the important point to remember is this: Man had a wonderful beginning. He came from the Creator's hand endowed with wonderful powers and possessing moral holiness. He appeared as the crown and goal of God's earthly creation.

All of this points to one inescapable conclusion. God made man for a great future—a high purpose. Man's dominion over the lower creation demonstrates his absolute separation from the animal kingdom in origin, association, and destiny. A beast can never ascend to the level of a man. How easily, however, a man can virtually descend to the level of a beast (Ps 49:10; 2 Pe 2:12)!

Man's original creation shows that God loves man, has great plans for him, and wants to meet him in holy fellowship. The account of man's creation has an eloquent message to the twentieth century. "Man, you not only can meet God! God is *waiting* and *longing* to meet you! He created you in the first place for fellowship with Himself. He will never rest until you meet Him. You will never find rest until you do."

Man's Testing

The Scriptures teach that after creating man God subjected him to a state of trial to transform his *holy nature* into *holy character*. A test was run, as it were. Man had to be given an opportunity to function as a free moral agent. A right choice of obedience to God's command would have graduated his moral nature into a holy moral character. It was God's right to command (Gen 2:16-17), and man's duty to obey, in the test set-up.

As it turned out, man failed the test. He made the wrong choice and disobeyed God. His holy nature was defiled. As a result he became a morally sinful character. This condition involved himself and his descendants in the guilt of sin and the defilement of depravity.

But in the love and wisdom of God, man's probation was for his own highest development and ultimate good. It was absolutely necessary. Behind it lay God's wonderful purpose of human redemption, foreplanned by Him as a vital part of His high purpose for man (Eph 1:5; 1 Pe 1:2; Rev 13:8).

Man Became a Sinner

When man fell, he did not lose his personality, but he lost his holy nature. He became a sinner and came into threefold death—spiritual, physical, and eternal.

Spiritual death, which is separation of soul and spirit from God, was thrust upon man the moment he sinned. He lost communion with God. Physical death, a relentless process of physical disintegration culminating in the separation of the soul and spirit from the body, was also instituted. Man also became subject to the "second death," the lake of fire, the place of eternal separation from God.

The lake of fire will be the one isolation ward in the future sinless universe. It was prepared for the devil and his angels (Mt 25:41) but human beings will enter it on the ground of their repudiating the Gospel of God's salvation and casting their lot with Satan and his angels (Rev 20:10-15). This second death is the ultimate fate of sin and sinners.

Fallen man not only fell under the curse of sin and the resulting triple death, he also succumbed to the influence of Satan and demonic power (Col 1:13). Through man's sinful nature these evil spirit agencies could encourage and control him, egging him on in sin and rebellion against God.

Holy Scripture paints a realistic picture of the wickedness and depravity of fallen man and his lost estate apart from the grace and mercy of God. The divine verdict is that the whole world—including all of us— is guilty before God (Ps 14:1-3). God declares that as a result of man's fall, all mankind without exception is "under sin" (Ro 3:9). "There is none righteous, not even one" (Ro 3:10). "All have sinned and fall short of the glory of God" (Ro 3:23).

Every member of Adam's fallen race is pronounced as under God's judgment and guilty before God. Sinful man is utterly unable to do anything to merit favor or acceptance with God. He is excluded entirely from God's grace revealed in Christ.

What's to be done?

6

THE "GOODY-GOODY" PHILOSOPHY

Man is not stupid. He was created with intelligence.

He's smart enough to know that something is wrong, and he tirelessly attempts to do something about it.

The "goody-goody" philosophy has probably kept more people from God than even Communism. Goody-goody thinking supposes that man, the way he is, is good enough for God.

Man's failure to realize he is a fallen, lost creature unable to save himself, and his optimistic trust in his own supposed goodness, constitute the chief barriers that keep most people away from God. Pride and self-righteousness in the heart generate the most damaging form of self-deception. This fatally mistaken spirit insulates the soul against God. "For if anyone thinks he is something when he is nothing, he deceives himself" (Gal 6:3).

This is where so many are sidetracked into a blind alley and fail to get on the highway that leads to God.

They think they are sufficiently good, at least as good as most people. They evaluate themselves purely on the basis of human criteria. They completely lose sight of the fact that in the matter of approach to God they should be dealing with divine and not human standards.

One does not have to go far in gospel witness and soul-winning work to encounter the "goody-goody" form of self-deception. It is extremely common. Why? Because so many people shy away from a candid-camera shot of themselves. They have never faced up to their own real condition *before God.* Understandably, they avoid the comparison.

So many people look at themselves through the rose-tinted glasses of their own pride and self-esteem. What they see exists only in their own dream world. They refuse to look at themselves through the fine lens of God's Word to see themselves as they really are. Their vision of what is temporal is superficial and what is eternal is warped. They don't allow God's Word to x-ray the thoughts and intents of their hearts (Heb 4:12).

As a result the soul-winner is continually confronted with self-deluding nonsense as he attempts to present the Gospel to sinners.

One unsaved person excuses himself from the claims of the Gospel by asserting, "I believe that if I do the best I can and practice the golden rule, I'll go to heaven."

Another declares, "If I go to church and lead a

good moral life, I have just as good a chance of getting to heaven as the next person."

Another affirms, "I've been baptized and confirmed and I am staking my hope on these religious acts."

Another protests, "I belong to such-and-such church and lead a religious life. I expect someday to make heaven, if I hold out."

And so on, ad infinitum. The excuses for rejecting God's offer of salvation are endless. One becomes utterly weary of the substitutes offered by man's pride and self-delusion for the gift of eternal life that God extends hopefully and without price to every lost sinner.

Do Good People Go to Heaven?

The answer is, "Yes, good people go to heaven, provided there are any good people." But the Scriptures plainly declare that there just are no good people. The Scriptures tell us that there is not even so much as one good person on the face of the earth. "Indeed, there is not a righteous man on earth who continually does good and who never sins" (Ec 7:20, NASB).

In setting forth the Gospel of God, the apostle Paul under divine inspiration, declared that it is written (Ps 14:1-3; 53:1-4):

"THERE IS NONE RIGHTEOUS, NOT EVEN ONE;
THERE IS NONE WHO UNDERSTANDS,
THERE IS NONE WHO SEEKS FOR GOD;
ALL HAVE TURNED ASIDE,
TOGETHER THEY HAVE BECOME USELESS;

There is none who does good,
There is not even one"   (Ro 3:10-12).

What a contrast to the goody-goody philosophy! Obviously, God and man do not agree on the condition of man. Obviously, man's optimistic assessment of himself is unfounded if we are to believe God, and man is blinded to his true condition.

Man thinks he does "righteous" things—religion, morality, philanthrophy—but God calls these and all of man's other actions "filthy rags" (Is 64:6, KJV) when they are offered in place of faith.

Is God looking on the dark side? Not at all, when we consider that His own nature is our standard.

Is that fair, we ask. Yes, when God has made it possible through Christ for us to comply with His standard.

But actually we can eliminate man's claims to righteousness on ordinary earthly grounds. The human experience familiar to all of us clearly indicts each and every one of us. A man says, "I believe that if I do the best I can and treat everyone fairly I will go to heaven." But will he be able to back it up? Will his earthly life testify to an effective effort along these lines?

Let's be honest. The standard we've set for ourselves is too high. In complete sincerity, did anyone ever in his life do the best he could, treat everyone fairly, and really believe in his own heart that his moral system would please God?

Will the truly self-saved person please stand up?

It follows then that we, if we are trusting in our own good acts, are consigning ourselves to hell.

Heaven Is for Bad People!

That's right. Heaven is for bad people.

Heaven is for people so bad they cannot even help themselves. Heaven is for people who see themselves condemned before God, utterly lost and without hope apart from the grace of God revealed in Jesus Christ.

People who come to realize that their position with God is as bad as the Scriptures say it is flee to Christ the Saviour as their only hope. Such people are ready to accept the pardon God offers. Such offenders who realize themselves to be sinners thankfully receive the cleansing Christ's death provides. They trust Christ and are delivered from God's judgment. They are admitted to heaven not because they were so bad but because they *saw* themselves as being so bad, and took the only efficacious option.

Ironically, the "good people," those who are so righteous in their own sight that they do not feel they need a saviour, are condemned to hell. Those who trust in themselves, in their own goodness and works, their religion and morality, are found lacking the perfect righteousness God alone bestows. Those without Christ are offering only their own good graces. The Scripture is very clear; the offering won't be acceptable (Ro 3:26).

The gospel of Luke contains the inspiring story of Zacchaeus, the publican, who fully realized he was a sinner and needed the Saviour. When Jesus passed by in His travels, Zacchaeus did not let pride or a phony "goody-goody" complex hinder him from seeking the Lord.

This publican was unlike so many who miss life's greatest encounter—the meeting of God—simply because they are so sedate, so proper, so good, so proud. Jesus passes by, but they are too straight-laced to break with the crowd and run ahead to meet their Saviour as Zacchaeus did. They are too prim to scramble up a sycamore tree, as that convicted sinner did, to see the Saviour (Lk 19:1-8).

These goody-goody people (and the world is well supplied with them) never make contact with God. They never receive His matchless gift of forgiveness and eternal life. They never hear His wondrous words to Zacchaeus, "Today salvation has come to this house . . . for the Son of Man has come to seek and to save *that which was lost*" (Lk 19:9-10, emphasis added).

They fail to see, or do not wish to see, that God's grace is available to the guilty and the condemned, that God's salvation is for the lost, that divine forgiveness is extended to sinners exclusively.

They don't see that heaven is for bad people who receive God's remedy for their badness.

Such self-righteous persons may wonder why they never meet God. They think that He is seeking them —the good people—but simply has not found them for some reason. He is often pictured for them that way by liberal theologians.

But, of course, God is seeking the lost, and these people are constantly dodging Him by denying that they *are* the lost.

Games People Play with God

Unsaved people who protest their innocence before God, or who offer Him their self-styled goodness or morality as a substitute for His expressed preference, are playing hide-and-seek with Him. God is seeking them, but they are hiding behind a screen of self-righteousness.

It is not, of course, that God cannot see them where they are. He has already expressed that this goody-goodiness will not be sufficient. It would be hard to expect Him, after having advanced His wonderful plan of salvation at such cost, to search out people who subscribe to some other.

People also play a version of the game of tag with God. God is "It," and reaches out to touch people. If they are touched by Him, they will in turn become "It," and they can reach out and touch others.

But just as in the actual game, such people avoid being tagged and spend their lives avoiding God. They avoid even knowing the rules of the game.

Whatever game is played against God, it is very dangerous. Defeat must eventually be the result. Eternal hell will be the unavoidable penalty.

When a team plays a whole game and scores nothing, the game is called a shutout. This expresses the unbeliever's position for eternity.

Good News for Bad People

Gospel means "good news." The Christian Gospel is the good news that God has undertaken in His love and grace to rescue man from the awful plight into which he plunged when he listened to Satan and rebelled against his Creator. This originally happened back in the Garden of Eden.

Adam became conscious of his nakedness—sinfulness—after he ate from the tree, and he began what man has futilely tried to do ever since. He tried to cover his shame. He tried to make himself presentable to God. He "sewed fig leaves together" to hide his sin from God (Gen 3:7).

Adam knew it wasn't going to work when he "heard the sound of the Lord God walking in the garden in the cool of the day." He hid himself in fear and confusion. And fallen man has continued to hide from God, behind one tree or another, notwithstanding his constant application of fig leaves.

But at that electrifying moment when God appeared in the garden the grace of God began to operate on behalf of fallen man. The very first intimations of the Gospel appear. "Then the LORD God called to the man, and said to him, 'Where are you?'" (Gen 3:9).

The man was called to account for his sin and was not considered guiltless, but God on the spot offered a far-reaching remedy. God gave man good news. This good news has been called the *protevangelium,* "the first gospel."

> "And the Lord God said to the serpent . . . I will put enmity between you and the woman, and between your seed and her seed; he shall bruise you on the

head, and you shall bruise him on the heel" (Gen 3:14-15).

Here, if we understand the prophetic meaning of the passage, is the first record of the Gospel of God's grace. It characterizes a tremendous conflict between "the seed of the woman" (the virgin-born Christ) and "the seed of the serpent" (the devil-begotten Antichrist). Wounds will be received on both sides, but the Antichrist will suffer a fatal one. The wound of the seed of the woman of course, is not permanent, as Christ is resurrected. Actually it results on behalf of man in complete conquest over sin, hell, and the power of Satan.

The emphasis here is that the good news, presented so early in the affairs of men, is applicable only to those who, like Adam, feel their guilt and know their lostness. For those who have eaten of the tree and are willing to contest with God about it the Gospel is no good news at all.

So, clearly, we don't have to try to get ready for heaven. We'd do a very bad job. We merely turn ourselves over as we are to the Saviour. Believe, receive, rejoice; how simple it is. God planned it this way and wrote it out in His word. "These have been written that you may believe that Jesus is the Christ, the Son of God; and that believing you may have life in His name" (Jn 20:31).

It is important to realize that the Gospel offers salvation on the basis of faith and faith alone. "For by grace you have been saved through faith; and that not of yourselves, it is the gift of God; not as a result of works, that no one should boast" (Eph 2:8-9).

God Takes Charge

The events of the garden scene go on to show God immediately taking action as fallen man's advocate. He emphasized the good news of man's redemption and presented it vividly in object lesson form, much like a teacher inculcates a truth by using natural objects. God impressed it upon the eye and the mind indelibly and unforgettably.

Scarcely had the glorious prediction that the seed of the woman should bruise the serpent's head faded from the hearing of the first sinners of the human race than "the LORD God made garments of skin for Adam and his wife, and clothed them" (Gen 3:21). He covered their nakedness and shame.

Beautifully and simply God presented to the human race a picture of what the Gospel offers lost sinners. He might have made garments out of heavenly materials, but instead chose the skin of an earthly animal, which involved the shedding of blood. This typified the death of Christ as the ground of the sinner's forgiveness and salvation.

Man's sin is removed from God's sight by the garments, and God's pardon for man is illustrated as He covers him.

Clearly, all the action taken in this initial salvation was taken by God. Man did nothing but realize that he was in trouble and needed help. The lesson pertains vividly today.

Stick to the True Gospel

Salvation was designed to be a simple matter and it *is* simple according to the Gospel. But some men will not have things simple, and throughout the ages human efforts have been made to adulterate the Gospel.

God's Gospel is the Gospel of grace.

Salvation depends *solely* upon the grace of God in Christ. The moment the principle of human merit or works is introduced, even in the slightest degree, the Gospel ceases to be the true Gospel and becomes something else. It actually becomes "a different gospel; which is really not another" (Gal 1:6-7).

The Gospel is, in effect, a prescription which must be used in precisely the form prepared. It must be constantly guarded from distortion and perversion. The apostle realized this important fact when he warned, "But even though we, or an angel from heaven, should preach to you a gospel contrary to that which we have preached to you, let him be accursed" (Gal 1:8).

To emphasize the gravity of the peril, Paul reiterated, "As we have said before, so I say again now, if any man is preaching to you a gospel contrary to that which you received, let him be accursed" (Gal 1:9).

What a timely warning in the age of rampant occultism and widespread demon activity, when false

prophets and false cults are flourishing like rank
weeds in an uncultivated garden (1 Ti 4:1; 1 Jn
4:1). Never was the pure Gospel of grace so im-
perilled by perversion as in the abysmal religious confusion of these last days preceding the coming of the
Lord for His own.

Satan and demonic forces are making an all-out attack against the Christian Church. Their diabolical
aim is to introduce apostasy and heresy to divide and
discourage God's people. The chief strategy seems to
be the spawning of new cults to obscure the simplic-
ity and all-sufficiency of the Gospel.

Satan well knows that the success of the Gospel
spells his own undoing. He is making every effort to
deny the Gospel, or pervert it. Failing this, he attempts to blind men to its efficacy and confuse them
with alternatives.

God grant that we may all believe the simple Gospel in all its power and we may be diligent to defend
it, cherish it, and proclaim it gladly to others.

Let us always remember that the Christian Gospel
is the ultimate "good news" from God to man. Let us
enjoy it, believe it completely, and pass it on to others.
If you have never done so, accept the wonderful invitation of the Gospel. Start in the way to God by
trusting Jesus Christ as your Saviour.

7

SIN IN FOCUS

Many people today are not interested in such ideas as "sin" and "transgression." These concepts are old-fashioned and no longer valid, they feel. Thus they also cannot accept absolute standards of conduct.

But if we seriously want to encounter God, we're going to have to admit the reality of His concepts, beginning with sin.

It will be good for us. Dr. Karl A. Menninger, the famed psychiatrist who operates the Menninger Clinic, where he has treated many casualties of the new morality, has recently written a book called *Whatever Became of Sin.* Dr. Menninger asks, "Doesn't anyone believe in sin anymore?" His thesis is that when we lose our concept of sin, we lose something vital to the human psyche.[1]

Bishop Fulton J. Sheen calls this new absence of sin "emptying heaven of God," and says the biblical concept of what is "utterly sinful" (Ro 7:13) is being systematically excised from the consciousness of modern man.[2]

As far as present society is concerned, to cite the Ten Commandments and hold to eternally unchangeable moral principles is to revert to the horse-and-buggy days and outmoded ways of life. In today's world, even where God is nominally acknowledged and His moral laws are recognized, there is a deplorable insensitivity to sin. The Watergate scandal is a clear illustration that the common people do not have a corner on the sin market in the United States. Their leaders themselves practiced some of the new morality.

Immoral conduct pervades every sector of modern life.

We have said that God forgives sin, and truly, it is not men's sins that keep them away from God. It is rather refusing to face up to their sins. If, after all, we have finally forgotten what sin is, we will not know what a sinner is.

If someday man decides that it is normal to be covered with red spots, we can abolish the disease of measles. But even under this new morality of measles, those with red spots are going to feel sick.

What Is Sin?

Everybody ought to know what sin is. Also the consequences and the gravity of it.

Unbelievers cannot get to God without a sound

concept of sin, and believers fall into many pitfalls and snares of the devil because they don't understand what sin really is. Sin is a thing all of us have but few of us can define, at least according to God's definition.

Scripture reveals that all of us are born in sin and have from birth the depraved nature of Adam. King David declared this truth, so evident in human experience: "Behold, I was brought forth in iniquity, and in sin my mother conceived me" (Ps 51:5).

Fortunately the Holy Spirit, the ultimate Author of the Scriptures, has given us a complete diagnosis of this dreadful malady that has infected the entire race. He details the symptoms and prescribes the remedy. A rich and varied vocabulary is used to describe sin, both in the Hebrew Old Testament and the Greek New Testament. The Holy Spirit plainly reveals what sin is and warns us against its dire consequences.

The Old Testament and the New Testament agree on the definition of sin. The most commonly used Hebrew word, and the most commonly used Greek word, both mean in English "to miss the mark."

The picture is that of a man shooting or throwing at a target set up for him and consistently missing it. Man is made to "shoot for God." But what a contrast he is to the stone-slingers mentioned in Judges 20:16: "Out of all these people 700 choice men were left-handed; each one could sling a stone at a hair and not miss."

God is the true target or goal of life. Sin causes man to "miss" God and to live at odds with Him. Sin spells man's failure to meet the divine standard.

"There is no man who does not sin" (1 Ki 8:46).
"For all have sinned and fall short of the glory of
God" (Ro 3:23).

Interestingly, ancient pagans, while not appreciat-
ing the distinctive biblical meaning of sin, held similar concepts of it. The Greeks regarded their offences
as shortcomings and called them *harmartiai,* or "bad
shots." They accurately described the concept of sin,
but just didn't appreciate the seriousness of "missing
the mark." They regarded their shortcomings as
bound to happen and best forgotten. It was useless, in
their estimation, to spend time in regretting bad shots.

But the Bible, in its revelation of the infinitely holy
God, does not present these "misses" as mere miscal-
culations or failures, but as serious violations against
our very nature. And these sins are punishable by
death.

Sin Is Trespassing

Sin is an overstepping of the commandments of
God, an intrusion into a restricted area. It is a rebellious breaking through the divine fence between good
and evil. "They have transgressed My covenant, and
rebelled against My law" (Ho 8:1).

When the brother of the prodigal son declared that
he had never "transgressed" any of his father's commandments (Lk 15:29), he meant that he had stayed
within the expressed boundaries of his father's will.
The younger brother did not, and so had committed a
trespass.

The apostle James enunciated the fact that all of

us have transgressed the moral law of God, and as a result stand guilty. "For whoever keeps the whole law and yet stumbles in one point, he has become guilty of all. For He who said, 'DO NOT COMMIT ADULTERY,' also said, 'DO NOT COMMIT MURDER.' Now if you do not commit adultery, but do commit murder, you have become a transgressor of the law" (Ja 2:10-11).

Man is prone to look on the outside of the situation—to consider transgression purely as an outward violation of the law. He tends to overlook the fact that there are sins within the heart. Harboring hatred in the heart is tantamount to committing murder. Harboring lustful thoughts is equivalent to committing adultery, as Jesus pointed out (Mt 5:27-28).

Men also have an uncanny capacity to acclimatize to sin. The more they sin, the more sin they can tolerate. Sin tends to blind the sinner. It bewitches him so that what he once abhorred, and was positively nauseated at, he now accepts. What he once only tolerated, he now eagerly embraces. Sin is an addiction, and we are fast becoming a world of sin addicts.

Sin Is Lawlessness

Man has found by bitter experience that he really does need laws. Societies, small and large, formed on the basis of the natural goodness in men's hearts have only shown in the long run that laws are a better idea.

Iniquity is the biblical term for that which is not right toward God; it describes that which insults His deity. The vanity of idol worship, blasphemy, or ir-

religious conduct of any sort are examples (Job
34:36; Mt 7:23; Ac 8:22-23). Toward man, iniquity
includes any gross wrong or injustice. Everyone "who
names the name of the Lord," therefore, is to "de-
part from iniquity" (KJV), "abstain from wickedness" (2 Ti 2:19).

Lawlessness stresses the aspect of sin that flagrant-
ly violates all law, of both God and man. It particularly refers to infractions of the law of Moses, but includes the eternal moral law of God written on the
hearts of all men (Ro 2:14-15).

The direction the world is taking today prepares
the way for the coming of the Antichrist, the ultimate
lawbreaker (2 Th 2:8). This future world ruler will
be the supreme enemy of all law, whether of God or
men. He will "oppose" and "exalt himself above"
every god or object of worship "so that he takes his
seat in the temple of God," then, restored in Jerusalem, "displaying himself as being God" (2 Th 2:4).

The characters of Revelation—the Dragon (Satan), the Beast (the Antichrist), and the False
Prophet, and their henchmen—will be the climactic
expression of lawlessness in the end time.

Man is to discover, on a global level, the net results of society without law at the battle of Armaged-
don.

Sin Is Ignorance

Satan, the prince of this world, works hard at ob-
scuring definitions of sin. Earthly sinners are blinded

by Satan, and this is part of the reason why so many unsaved people remain unaware of their true condition before God. They do not understand their guilt, they do not sense their peril.

A sword hangs over their heads but they do not see it. They teeter frighteningly on the edge of an abyss, but they do not sense the danger. They are just a step away from eternity, a heartbeat away from hell, but they never stop to think about what they are doing.

The Bible considers ignorance to be sin. In other words, being ignorant of what we ought to know is no excuse for not knowing it. While many of the sins of the unsaved are done in ignorance, they are still sins, and separate them from the holy God.

God's grace, of course, provides for sins of ignorance as well as all other sins.

God provides for the errors of His own redeemed people. This was set forth in the Old Testament in the ritual on the Day of Atonement (Lev 16:15-16; Heb 9:7). The high priest was to offer a blood sacrifice for himself and for the sins of the people committed in ignorance, so that Israel could obtain atonement.

When Christ was being crucified He prayed for His very crucifiers, "Forgive them; for they do not know what they are doing" (Lk 23:34). Peter, in showing the Jews their guilt in rejecting Messiah, referred to their sin of ignorance: "And now, brethren, I know that you acted in ignorance, just as your rulers did also" (Ac 3:17). But their ignorance, he taught, did not expiate the sin or remove the guilt.

The apostle Paul declared that his early career as a persecutor of Christians was the result of the sin of ignorance. God saved him and called him into service despite his having been "a blasphemer, a persecutor, and a violent aggressor." Yet he states, "I was shown mercy, because I acted ignorantly in unbelief" (1 Ti 1:13).

Ignorance was forgiven in all of these cases, when the proper approach to God was made, but it is clear that without the proper approach to God, ignorance is just another sin.

Sin Is Unbelief

Unbelief is a special kind of sin. It is sin in an aggravated degree. It is an insult to the truthfulness of God. It refuses to believe what God says.

The apostle John explains that unbelief calls God a liar: "The one who does not believe God has made Him a liar, because he has not believed in the witness that God has borne concerning His Son" (1 Jn 5:10).

Unbelief springs from the old corrupt nature. "Take care, brethren, lest there should be in any one of you an evil, unbelieving heart, in falling away from the living God" (Heb 3:12). Unbelief causes the believer to lose fellowship with God and become ensnared in vain idolatry—faith in materialism and selfishness.

It is unbelief that shuts the door to heaven and opens the door to hell. Unbelief rejects God's Word and refuses salvation through Christ. Unbelief declines to meet God as the ultimate need of life and instead chooses the pleasures of the senses and materialistic wealth.

Unbelief lies behind men's fabrications about God —those convenient concepts that so well fit superficial needs. If one does not believe in the true God, then one is free to form any god that suits his purposes.

Unbelief stands squarely between man and God, and is the most effective device for defeating the sufficiency of Christ's sacrifice.

Where Did Sin Come From?

One thing is sure—sin didn't come from God. He originally created a sinless universe with sinless creatures to inhabit it. He did not create sin or sinners.

Before making man, God created angels. These ethereal creatures were also created as free moral agents. As self-determining personalities they could choose to obey their Creator and remain sinless, or disobey and become sinners.

Lucifer, the highest and most glorious of God's angels, chose to disobey (Is 14:12-14). He became the first sinner. He introduced sin into a sinless universe. Sin transformed him into Satan, the adversary of God.

A great segment of the angelic community followed Satan in disobedience (Rev 12:4). These rebels became the fallen angels, or demons.

All of this happened before God created man and

placed him on the earth. How long ago this revolution took place we do not know. But there are scriptural intimations that it occurred in connection with this planet in its pristine glory, "when the morning stars sang together, and all the sons of God shouted for joy" (Job 38:7).

The "sons of God" are angels. Their shouts of joy celebrated the laying of the earth's cornerstone. The rejoicing was likely occasioned by the unbroken fellowship of sinless creatures with their Creator, before sin entered the universe.

8

THE FATE OF THE SINNER

Understanding the pre-history of the world we see that things didn't really begin with the creation of the earth, or man, as even many Bible believers think. Man entered an arena in which conflict had already been established.

God certainly meant well when He created man. He created us in His own image as holy, righteous personalities. Scripture explicitly reveals that God did not create man a sinner. Man became a sinner by his own choice. He disobeyed God (Gen 2:17; 3:6; Ro 5:19), succumbing to Satan's deception and enticement.

We have Satan, not God, to blame for our state of sin.

How Did It Happen that **Every** Human Being Became a Sinner?

You may say, "All right, Adam was a sinner. But I, personally, did not eat from any forbidden tree. How did *I* become a sinner?"

Scripture teaches that Adam's sin was imputed, or judicially reckoned, to the whole race. Romans 5:12-

21 declares that all men sinned when Adam, the father of our race, sinned. As a result, all men incurred the penalty of physical death. "Therefore, just as through one man sin entered into the world, and death through sin, and so death spread to all men, because all sinned" (Ro 5:12).

Death, then, is the characteristic result of sin. We can see that every man died during the period between Adam and Moses (that is, before the Mosaic law was given), and then all men continued to die, with the exception of Enoch and Elijah, who were translated without physical death for a special divine purpose and in prospect of Christ's redemptive work.

Of course people who, in effect, have no sins, such as infants and imbeciles, die also. Certainly they have never sinned willfully, as Adam did, so that the imputation of sin to the entire race is not a matter of personal sins on the part of each individual. Personal sins, and their consequences, are another matter. These are remitted on the basis of Christ's salvation. That persons such as infants and imbeciles come under the grace of God, is evident from Scripture. All men were made saveable as a result of Christ's death, and we believe that those who do not reach accountability come under the benefits of that salvation.

Those who do reach accountability, however, must believe the Gospel to be saved.

You may ask, "Is God just in passing along to all men the sins of Adam?" The answer lies in the nature of man and the nature of God. We have already seen that His infinite holiness brooks no relationship with sin, and that each of us is conceived by sinful parents, as King David pointed out, reaching all the way back to the garden. God must be just.

Looking on the brighter side, we can appreciate God's provision of salvation for those who believe in Christ.

In the matter of personal sins, however, God deals with both sinners, and saints on the basis of their deeds or works. Sinners are punished accordingly in hell; saints are rewarded, or deprived of rewards, in heaven.

Why Did God Permit All This?

Our omniscient God must have known where the world was heading when He created it. Why did He let us in for all the misery occasioned by sin?

The Creator, of course, foreknew the Fall and fore-planned His great redemptive program for men. He chose the earth as the arena for His contest with Satan to show the entire universe how He would deal with sin and sinners.

Evidently it was in connection with the earth that sin began among Lucifer and his angels. Thus, in this great drama, God utilized the earth to make a special order of beings called "man." God would use man and his Fall to demonstrate to all intelligent creatures how He, an infinitely holy and loving Creator, would deal with sin and rebellion.

The plan, calling forth the vast redemptive spec-tacle in which God, in Christ, actually became a man, is divinely designed to accomplish wondrous things. The accomplishment of the redemption of a free moral creature will last throughout eternity. God's grace and love will be proclaimed in the success of this demonstration.

The divine goal of a sinless universe will be realized through the population of Adam's many sons brought to glory (Heb 2:10). After the curtain of time is lifted and eternity dawns in splendor, these vast multitudes, saved and glorified from the fallen race of men, will join the myriads of holy angels who never fell. Together they will populate what we usually call "heaven," by which we mean a new heaven, a new earth, and a new Jerusalem on the earth, together with a universe cleansed from sin.

But God's holiness and severity with sin will be magnified in a special way. The universe can only become "sin-cleansed" through the isolation and confinement of all sinners. Satan and the fallen angels, as well as unrepentant sinners of the human family, will therefore be consigned to gehenna, eternal hell (Rev 20:11-15).

Never again will sin or any sinner cast a shadow over the eternal light and bliss of God's well-planned eternal state. The plan is already in motion and no one—neither the devil, nor his demons, nor rebellious men—can in any way arrest its progress.

From Scripture we get a picture of our God moving inexorably forward, progressing steadily to perfect His mighty creation according to the infinite wisdom revealed in His glorious plan. Some of us may shrink from the thought of being part of an audio-visual demonstration. But remember, that final perfected eternity is available to us all. While we are now mere mortal men and not angels, we have every chance through God's redemptive grace to share the ultimate creation of the perfect Creator.

Nowhere is the onward march of our God better pictured than in a hymn we've sung for one hundred years, perhaps without thinking about the words:

> Mine eyes have seen the glory of the coming
> of the Lord;
> He is trampling out the vintage where the grapes
> of wrath are stored;
> He hath loosed the fateful lightning of His
> terrible swift sword,
> His truth is marching on.
>
> Glory, glory Hallelujah!
> Glory, glory Hallelujah!
> Glory, glory Hallelujah!
> His truth is marching on.
>   JULIA WARD HOWE

Plain Old Willful Sin

Many people don't think sin is very serious. People refuse to face up to God's estimate of sin, and as we have said, this keeps them away from God.

We have mentioned the Greeks and their concept of "bad shots." People today are still shooting just as badly.

The unsaved religionist views sin as little more

than a well-intentioned mistake. The cultist views it as a mere error of the mortal mind. Self-righteous folks look upon sin as nothing more than a natural infirmity, a kind of disease for which they in no way deserve punishment. The libertine, or completely uncontrolled sinner, holds that sin is an amiable weakness for which he is not blameworthy at all.

The natural man, who does not follow any formal religion, estimates sin as a hazard of life, like any accident. The Christian fatalist makes out sin to be an ever-present necessity, a sort of carcass he must drag around with him. He expects no victory over it in this life.

However the estimations may go, one thing is clear. In order to approach God, one must understand sin as what He says it is. There must be a solid and unrelenting conviction that sin is the sad and terrible reality of being separated utterly from God.

Jenkin Lloyd Jones, the distinguished journalist, said in an address to the American Society of Newspaper Editors, "It's time we hit 'the sawdust trail.' It's time we revive the idea that there is such a thing as sin—just plain old willful sin, It's time we brought self-discipline into style."[1]

Those who underestimate the seriousness of sin, of course, are bad candidates for salvation, as we have pointed out. Throw a drowning man a life preserver and he will grab it and be rescued. But throw a man standing on solid ice the same life preserver and he won't be interested.

This refusing the preserver may be fatal, however,

if it turns out that he is standing on the proverbial "thin ice."

The Wages of Sin

The Bible says that the wages of sin is death.

We have already said that sin is very serious, but we should go on to say that if the cure is not applied it is fatal.

Sin may be compared to a disease that is potentially fatal but which, with proper diagnosis and remedy, can be cured. All of us have contracted the disease, thus all of us need the cure.

Even in the case of a believer, persistent scandalous sin eventuates in physical death (1 Co 5:1-5). The physical life of the believer is terminated prematurely, so that his spirit might be saved (1 Co 11:30-32; 1 Jn 5:16). With the unbeliever, sin results in eternal death since he has not claimed Christ's cure. Eternal death, as we have said, means everlasting separation from God. It is more than physical death. It is the death of the soul and spirit as well.

Obviously, God's salvation plan is more than a way for men to achieve a more satisfying life. It is in fact a cure—the only known remedy—for death.

"I came that they might have life," said Jesus (Jn 10:10).

The Penalty for Sin

We experience penalties for our sins.

On the human plane the penalty is the suffering

which is imposed as a punishment for the commission of a crime or other offense. On the divine plane the penalty is essentially the reaction of God's holiness against sin.

God turns His back on sin. There is no element of hate or vengeance in God's dealings with men. God is not a peevish tyrant venting His spleen against those who have displeased Him. Nor is He a vengeful deity, spitefully getting even with those who have offended Him. He is, in fact, infinite love (1 Jn 4:8). But He is infinite love expressing itself in infinite holiness (Is 6:3).

God's reaction toward sin is, therefore, the result of both His infinite love and His infinite holiness. It is characterized sometimes by anger, even great wrath (Zec 1:15; Ro 1:18; Rev 15:7). But these terms, so familiar to the human emotional response, don't imply anything less than the infinite perfection of deity. God's anger and wrath describe a holy Creator's response to evil, but we must bear in mind too, that His plan of salvation applies to all sinners, on all levels of sin equally. He has expressed, along with His anger and wrath, His desire that no man should perish.

The object of God's penalizing sin is not to reform the sinner, but rather to vindicate the unchangeably holy character of God.

Sin exacts a penalty in this life as well as the life to come. In fact, theologians sometimes employ the term "moral penalty" to describe the natural consequences of sin in this life. The terms "positive" or "judicial" penalty, on the other hand, denote the penalty of sin as it applies to the life to come.

The difference between moral penalty and positive or judicial penalty becomes clear in a typical family situation. A father may forbid his child to play on a dangerous rock ledge, specifying that the child will lose all playing privileges for a week if he breaks this rule. The child then plays on the ledge anyway and falls and breaks his leg.

The pain and the period of healing represent our "moral penalty," which follows naturally from the child's disobedience. The positive or judicial penalty comes later when the child is well again. The father originally specified a penalty for breaking the given rule, and if he is just he must now enforce it. The child forfeits his playing privilege now because that was the penalty originally attached to the offense.

The father's love for his child is certainly not at issue here, of course. The father may be angry and wrathful, but even as he applies the penalty he looks only toward the greatest good for his child.

It is evident that the natural consequences of transgression constitute a part—but only a part—of the penalty for sin. The judicial aspect of penalty contains a personal element and must satisfy the holy wrath of the law-Giver and Judge. This latter aspect of the penalty for sin will only be realized in the life to come. The former, of course, is realized immediately in this life.

Various kinds of sins have their own moral penalties. Sensual sins are punished by the deterioration of the body, and spiritual sins by the corruption of the soul. Remorse of conscience is a distinctive part of the moral penalty of sin.

The penalty of sin as it affects the human race is threefold death. Spiritual death is separation of man's spirit from God, a state into which everyone is born (Lk 15:24; Eph 2:1). Physical death is separation of the soul from the body (Jn 11:14; Ac 2:24). Eternal death is separation of the spirit from God forever.

This last is actually spiritual death continued after physical death. It is realized for eternity in gehenna (Rev 20:11-15).

Let's Get Rid of Hell

Hell isn't very popular today.

The idea of eternal punishment is pretty much being done away with under the new morality. The biblical teaching on hell is being met with more and more skepticism and rejection. To a generation that boasts of its "emancipation" from moral codes and traditional modes of conduct, hell is becoming repulsive and unpalatable.

It is becoming customary to laugh off the whole idea as some kind of joke.

But the serious student of the Bible knows how utterly impossible it is to just do away with the truth of hell. It is linked up inescapably with the truths of heaven, God, the Gospel, salvation, and every other doctrine taught by the Word of God. These great teachings intertwine in the Scriptures so that eliminating one becomes impossible without destroying the others. Regardless of how inconvenient it may be, hell is here to stay, along with all of the more positive aspects of God's Word.

The issue is not, of course, whether we like the idea of hell or not, nor even its reality or unreality. The issue is the authority of the Bible—what God has said on the matter.

God's revelations are not open to questions by men.

Who's Going to Hell?

Most people miss the fact that hell was not prepared for human beings. It was in fact prepared for the devil and his fallen angels, or demons (Mt 25: 41). Hell became necessary to insure an eventual sinless eternity long before man was created on the earth and fell into sin.

When man succumbed to Satan, hell became necessary for him, since God's goal of a sinless universe will not be thwarted by wicked angels or unrepentant men. Man believed the devil, and the devil sold him a ticket to hell.

When God's creatures, endowed with the prerogative of free will, abuse that priceless privilege, they will be quarantined for eternity in one isolation ward for all sinners. They shall not be free to interfere with God's grand purpose—to establish a sinless order.

Hell is there so that heaven can be there. They stand or fall together. One is impossible without the other. Hell is God's way of solving the difficulty of sin in His universe. Heaven is His way of providing a wholly sinless environment.

Who, then, will go to hell? The answer is Satan, the fallen angels or demons, and all of the human race who fail to accept the provisions of salvation.

Hell Is for Good People

We said earlier that heaven is for bad people. In the same sense, hell is for good people.

It is taken for granted by most people, even many professing Christians, that bad people are going to hell. "How could it be otherwise?"

Of course it is true that bad people are going to hell. But many receive a jolt when they become aware of the fact that many "good" people are going there, too. These "good" people are all unsaved. They have never really trusted Christ or received salvation (Jn 3:5, 16).

Obviously, there are many kind, religious, philanthropic, moral people who are not regenerated Christians at all. They exist in Christianity, in non-Christian religions, and in circles where no religion is followed at all.

Now if the Gospel proclaimed salvation by works instead of by faith, then all these people would be saved. If God were not so infinitely holy and sin not so exceedingly evil, then God could allow enough latitude to receive these "good" people into heaven. And if heaven were for good people instead of for poor lost sinners saved by grace, then these people might have a chance to enter.

But, as things stand, "good" people presenting their merit, good deeds, and self-effort have no claim whatsoever upon God's grace and heaven. Those who in this life trust in their own goodness have, of course, no need to accept Christ, in their own estimation, and they omit the all-important step of receiving Him. They typically do not approach the question of salvation at all, but feel that they will somehow muddle through without it.

We stressed earlier that God must be met as He is. These "good" people, lacking knowledge of who God is and what He has said, have wasted all their efforts toward goodness in this life. They have neglected to face up to themselves as they really are. They have shied away from facing their sin and guilt.

They will repent at leisure.

The notorious juvenile deliquent protests to the judge in Juvenile Court, "I ain't no bad kid. I wash my face every day." His view of morality is very prevalent today. He may really believe that his innocence is based on a clean face, and it *is* a good idea for him to wash it every day. And the law does permit consideration of extenuating circumstances, character, and so forth in deciding the penalty for a criminal act.

But a clean face isn't an extenuating enough circumstance to excuse the crime. The boy will go to a detention center and repent at leisure.

Jesus said pointedly to an audience of self-righteous religionists of His day, "It is not those who are well who need a physician, but those who are sick. I have not come to call righteous men but sinners to repentance" (Lk 5:31-32).

The British essayist and historian Thomas Carlyle (1795-1881) concluded that the greatest of faults is to be conscious of none.

The Punishments in Hell

Hell will be a populous place, and no doubt some people reading this are on their way there. So we should discuss a little of what will go on there as described in God's Word.

Many people who believe in hell, who hold that wicked pepole must go there, have the hazy notion that all will be punished alike with essentially the same severity. However, it is obvious that unsaved people vary in quality of living fully as much as saved people. Saved people are going to be rewarded, Scripture tells us, for their fidelity in Christian living and service (cf. 1 Co 3:9-15 and 2 Co 5:10). It follows that punishment in hell will be by degrees also.

Both truths are consonant with God's character, absolutely fair and impartial, and man's experience of the differences in quality in the lives of both saved and unsaved persons (Ro 2:5; Rev 20:12-13; Mt. 16:27).

Jesus taught the principle of punishment according to the seriousness of the crime in the parable of the servants (Lk 12:41-48): "And that slave who knew his master's will and did not get ready or act in accord with his will, shall receive many lashes, but the one who did not know it, and committed deeds worthy of a flogging, will receive but few. And from everyone who has been given much shall much be required; and to whom they entrusted much, of him they will ask all the more" (vv. 47-48).

The apostle Paul warns sinners that God "will render to every man according to his deeds" (Ro 2:6; cf. Ps 62:12; Mt 16:27). "For there is no partiality with God" (Ro 2:11).

At the end of time, everybody who ever lived will stand before Christ. This vast concourse of the unsaved who have lived between creation and the end of the millennium will be judged at the Great White Throne "from the things which were written in the books, *according to their deeds*" (Rev 20:12; emphasis added).

This truth is repeated in the next verse:

"And they were judged, every one of them *according to their deeds*" (Rev 20:13, emphasis added).

According to the Bible, the quality of life led by the unsaved person is crucial to his experience in hell. The penalties will vary with the crimes. Likewise, the saved person will experience greater or lesser rewards in heaven, according to the life of service that he led.

What Will Hell Be Like?

Will there really be a fork-tailed devil in a red suit roasting howling victims over an open flame?

Actually, that picture is man-made and is not Scriptural. The pain, remorse, and suffering of hell will be real, we gather from the biblical accounts, but it will not be that of a destructible physical body suffering torments that we can identify.

After the second resurrection, all human beings get new bodies. The saved will be outfitted to exist forever in a sin-cleansed universe. The unsaved get a body which is also indestructible but subject to the misery of gehenna.

The red devil and roasting fire picture of the eternal torment of hell is probably not accurate in detail, since the supernatural—not the natural—realm is to be reckoned with; but we must conclude on sound scriptural bases that hell will be an unpleasant place to say the least.

Louis Untermeyer's poem, "Caliban in the Coal Mines," pictures tired miners remonstrating with God about His relatively comfortable position in heaven:

> God, we don't like to complain;
>   We know that the mine is no lark.
> But—there's the pools from the rain.
>   But—there's the cold and the dark.
>
> God, you don't know what it is—
>   You, in Your well-lighted sky—
> Watching the meteors whiz;
>   Warm, with the sun always by.
>
> God, if You had but the moon
>   Stuck in your cap for a lamp,
> Even You'd tire of it soon,
>   Down in the dark and the damp.

Nothing but blackness above
  And nothing that moves but the cars;
God, if You wish for our love,
  Fling us a handful of stars.

The poet imagines that God in His "well-lighted sky," does not realize the plight of those "down in the dark and the damp." But God, who placed the ore in the earth in the first place, is well aware of what it takes to extract it.

In a larger sense, God does realize that for those blinded by Satan there is "Nothing but blackness above."

But the grand and glorious message of the Gospel that rings down the corridors of time is this: God does want our love. In our darkness and need, deep in the coal mines of sin, He remembers us.

In Christ He has flung us "a handful of stars," but more than that, he offers us a heartful of peace, a life full of joy, an eternity full of fellowship with Himself.

Will you accept His gracious offer?

There's Room at the Cross for You

We would be remiss to conclude this section on sin without saying just once more that no one has to be subject to its ultimate results.

There's room at the cross for everyone. In His earthly ministry Jesus walked among sinners of all kinds—thieves, murderers, blasphemers, prostitutes. He had time for everyone. He patiently and lovingly taught the Gospel of salvation to the Samaritan woman in her ignorance. He explained the cosmic terms of God's plan for redemption to the scholar Nicodemus. He paused many times in His busy travels to touch a man sick with leprosy, lame or blind, and amid a welter of steady criticism, rendered him whole again.

And ultimately, He laid down His life for His friends, you and me included.

Sin is real. Sin is not relative, but has been defined clearly by Scripture. Its ultimate end is all too clearly defined also.

Think it over.

9

ONLY BELIEVE

This is the do-or-die chapter. This is where we talk about how to be saved.

Up to this point we've talked about how the world is today, and that in spite of everything, God still meets people in thrilling, life-changing encounters. We've talked about the nature of God so that we understand just who it is we are to meet. We've talked about you and everybody else, and how they really are. And we've talked about sin, the condition we all share.

Now it's time to put all this together and find a good use for it.

Presumably, if you have believed what we have said about God, you, and sin, you realize that you need to be saved. You shouldn't have to be coaxed. A drowning man does not have to be argued into being rescued. A hungry man does not have to be urged to eat. A tired man does not have to be convinced to rest.

So Great a Salvation!

Salvation is the event of a lifetime to say the least. The writer to the Hebrews calls it "so great a salvation" (Heb 2:3). Anyone who has experienced it can testify to his enthusiasm. Scripture shows that salvation is a work of all time—planned in eternity past, worked out in time, and having its prime effects in eternity future (Eph 1:4-6; Rev 13:8; Jn 1:29; Ro 5:8; Rev 13:5).

Salvation is, of course, God's work, not man's (Ps 3:8; Jon 2:9), and involves the triune God.

God the Father "has blessed us with every spiritual blessing in the heavenly places in Christ" (Eph 1:3). He chose us in Christ. He predestined us in Him "to adoption as sons." He did this to magnify His glorious grace which "He freely bestowed on us" in Christ, "the Beloved" (Eph 1:3-6).

God the Son in this great salvation has redeemed us through His blood and secured "the forgiveness of our trespasses" by His death on the cross (Eph 1:7). In dying for us, Christ reconciled us to God (2 Co 5:20-21). His death enabled the infinitely holy God to be propitious toward sinners. It not only made sinners savable, but enabled God to act on the plan—to save those who believe the Gospel. More than that, it enabled Him to cleanse the sinning saint—the already-saved sinner—on the basis of the confession of his sins (1 Jn 1:9; 2:2).

God the Holy Spirit likewise has an important ministry in this great salvation. He prepares the sinner to receive it by convicting him of his sin and need of forgiveness, and of the imputed righteousness of God (Jn 16:8-11). He works this salvation in the convicted sinner, whom He directs to believe in the Saviour.

The Holy Spirit regenerates the sinner who believes on Christ (Jn 3:3-5), at the same time baptizing him into vital union with Christ and with other believers (Ro 6:3-4). Also at the same moment, the Holy Spirit indwells the believer (1 Co 6:19), sealing him to the day of full redemption (Eph 4:30) and giving him the privilege of continual indwelling (Eph 5:18).

The Holy Spirit, in doing all this the moment the sinner is saved, thereby sets the believer in the sphere of spiritual fullness, because He places him "in Christ" in whom all the fullness dwells and in whom all completeness resides (Col 2:9-10).

With all of this work already done, not much is left for a human being to do to claim salvation.

HOW TO BE SAVED

Believe in Jesus Christ.

By Faith Alone

That's right. A complete list of God's requirements for entering His eternal plan of salvation would involve only one item—faith in Christ.

By faith and faith alone are we saved.

Salvation in all its limitless magnitude is secured, so far as human responsibility is concerned on the *one* condition of believing in Christ as Saviour. Believing is receiving.

To this one requirement no other obligation may be added without violating the Gospel of grace. To add any other stipulation is "deserting Him who called you by the grace of Christ" and taking up with "a different gospel which is really not another" but a distortion of "the gospel of Christ" (Gal 1:6-7).

To intrude some form of human works or merits into the Gospel of salvation is to do violence to clear scriptural teaching (Jn 3:16; Eph 2:8-9) and to totally disrupt the essential doctrine of salvation by grace alone (Titus 3:4-5), which is the heart of the Gospel (Titus 2:11-14).

By the very nature of the case, salvation is that which can be wrought by God alone, and solely on the principle of sovereign grace. Salvation is a work of God and in no sense an attainment of man. To introduce some form of human works with supposed merit is to attempt to do what only God Himself can do and has done through Christ.

Every feature involved in salvation presents an undertaking which is superhuman. To be accomplished at all, the whole transaction must be performed by God alone. Man must realize that the only relation he can sustain to this great transaction, once setting it in motion by his faith, is to depend on God to work it out in him.

Salvation through faith begins with those mighty

transformations that make a Christian what he is. It involves forgiveness of sins: past, present, and future. It guarantees the safekeeping of the believer. It assures him of eventual glorification and full conformity to Christ at the resurrection.

It promises a home in heaven.

"Only Believe"

Faith + nothing = salvation.

It seems so simple, and it is. But the apostle Paul, in his second letter to the church at Corinth, stressed that Satan would blind unbelievers to this simple truth (2 Co 4:4). He also deceives believers, to sully their full freedom and joy in Christ (Gal 1:6-7).

He has been successful to some measure. The Lord's own people are divided on doctrines, misguided into cults, and stunted in Christian growth by legalism and other errors. And there is vast misunderstanding among believers of the simple procedure for salvation. Some of the church have been guilty of professing an "amplified" Gospel—one that adds other requirements to faith.

Instead of "only believe"—the true Gospel message—we hear "repent and believe," "believe and be baptized," "believe and profess Christ," "believe and crown Christ as Lord," "believe and confess sin," or "believe and implore God to save you," etc.

At best, amplified gospels amount to wrong directions. A person may still get to the destination, but at some inconvenience. At worst, an amplified gospel is a perverted gospel—a denial of the true Gospel, in effect, a false gospel. The apostle invoked a double curse on false gospels because they set aside the true way of salvation and substitute a false way that precludes salvation (Gal 1:6-9).

In the following sections, we will deal with the most widely known amplified gospels and the failings of each in the light of God's true plan.

"Repent and Believe"

Repentance for sins, conceived as a separate act, is most commonly added to faith as a requirement for salvation. But Scripture in more than 150 passages, including all the great gospel invitations (e.g., Jn 3:16), limit the human responsibility to faith.

The fact is, repentance does not have to be *added* to faith—it is actually inseparable from it. Faith can never exist without repentance. To repent is to admit oneself a lost sinner.

There are many penitent, unsaved people. They feel sorry about their sins. But without faith in Christ they remain unsaved.

Repentance, alone, never saved anybody, and faith without repentance is inconceivable.

Repentance is actually a prerequisite for true faith. It puts the sinner in a state of heart and mind to be receptive to faith in the Gospel. But it is neither sufficient in itself, nor a requirement for salvation.

But the message of Christ causes repentance. Clearly, one cannot turn to Christ from something else without incurring this change of mind—toward God, toward himself, toward sin.

The turning to Christ equals faith, and faith equals salvation.

"Believe and Be Baptized"

Water baptism is a valid and important act of obedience and testimony to be performed *after* one is saved. But it is frequently made a requirement.

Two passages of Scripture have commonly been used to teach baptismal regeneration—the idea that baptism is mandatory to being saved. The first, Mark 16:16, says, "He who has believed and has been baptized shall be saved; but he who has disbelieved shall be condemned." The other is Peter's statement at Pentecost; "Repent, and let each of you be baptized in the name of Jesus Christ for the forgiveness of your sins; and you shall receive the gift of the Holy Spirit" (Ac 2:38).

The quotation from Mark, it should be said, occurs in a passage not found in the oldest and best manuscripts and is therefore suspect. In any case, a number of commentators interpret the term *baptized* in this Scripture as referring to Spirit baptism, or real baptism (Mt 3:11), rather than to water or ritual baptism.

L. S. Chafer, for one, follows the interpretation that baptism here is the reality and not the ritual: "The form of speech which this text presents is common in the Bible, namely that of passing from the main sub-

ject to one of the features belonging to that subject."
Chafer cites Luke 1:20 as an example: "Thou shalt
be dumb, and not able to speak" (KJV). The word
"dumb" is merely amplified by "not able to speak."
In our Mark Scripture, "has believed" is amplified by
the phrase "and is baptized," with reference to real
baptism.[1]

The passage in Acts has a peculiar time setting and
context that must be taken into consideration. Peter
was addressing the Jews in Jerusalem, where Jesus
had been crucified only a few weeks before. Obviously a drastic change of mind was essential here. The
water baptism would serve as an outward sign of the
inward faith inspired in those who could be considered the least likely to believe. Their receiving the
Holy Spirit meant they would be saved with the
common grace-faith salvation of the new era, then
being inaugurated.

In no other Scripture can baptism be reasonably
construed as a requirement for salvation, whereas
there is great emphasis on the idea of "faith plus
nothing."

"Believe and Confess Christ"

Public acknowledgement of Christ is the duty and
privilege of those who are saved, but it can never be
presented as a condition for salvation. Such a view
would be allowing a work of merit to intrude in the
area where God's work alone is sufficient.

To claim that a public confession of Christ is required for salvation is to discount the salvation of many people under circumstances which preclude such an act (e.g., in Russia).

Confession of Christ is wonderful as the expression of the *effect* of salvation, but it should not be confused with the *process* of salvation. Romans 10:9-10 puts it: "That if you confess with your mouth Jesus as Lord, and believe in your heart that God raised Him from the dead, you shall be saved; for with the heart man believes, resulting in righteousness, and with the mouth he confesses, resulting in salvation."

That is, the newly saved person makes confession of the fact that salvation has already occurred in his soul by faith. Faith results in the believer's "righteousness" before God. Confession attests that salvation before men.

"Believe and Crown Christ Lord"

This amplified gospel requires service, or discipleship, for salvation. It is not enough, according to this reasoning, for the individual to simply trust Christ as his sin-bearer. He must also evidence a life of service.

The purveyors of this thinking are trying to avoid "easy believism," which does contain some peril, but they rob salvation of its character as a free gift.

Again the error is in making some human merit enter the picture of salvation, and this, as we have seen, impinges on the purity of the Gospel of grace.

There is no more piously subtle abrogation of the Gospel than to tell a sinner that he must not only believe in the Saviour, but dedicate himself to do God's will, crown the Saviour Lord of his life, etc., etc. Obviously, dedication and service are highly desirable, but they are the privilege and the duty of the saved, never a condition of salvation for the unsaved (cf. Ro 12:1-2).

It is patently unfair to impose the Lordship of Christ and the rigid requirement of discipleship upon the unsaved. They have no ability or understanding to respond to such a call. God's call is strictly to the saving grace of Christ.

Even saved people, who possess new natures and the indwelling Spirit, find the rigors of discipleship the ultimate challenge.

"Believe and Confess Sin"

Here the notion is that sin must be confessed or restitution made before one can be saved. This philosophy is all too prevalent among certain groups of zealous, but badly taught Christians.

This amplified gospel rests on the fallacy that salvation is only for good people. The sinner, it is suggested, must divest himself of all that is evil before God will save him. He must qualify for salvation. He must be worthy of it.

At bottom, this view holds that God is not propitious toward sin, despite Christ's death. It also implies that the unregenerate person is able to improve his fallen condition. Human merit again finds its way into the picture of salvation.

But we have already seen that God is propitious toward the lost and justifies fully the ungodly (Ro 4:5). No one needs to improve himself to qualify for salvation since men were "enemies, sinners, and helpless" (Ro 5:6-10) when Christ died for them. All of men's failings are accounted for in Christ's death.

Actually, reformation follows salvation automatically, but the work is in God's province, not man's. It is the duty of the saved to confess their sins to restore fellowship with God (1 Jn 1:9), but this has no reference to salvation, of course.

Setting things right in one's life and making proper restitution wherever appropriate, is surely a Christian's solemn responsibility. This should never be neglected. But it is hardly the means of salvation.

Zacchaeus, the tax collector, presented a heartening testimony to his salvation when he told the Lord, "Behold, Lord, half of my possessions I will give to the poor, and if I have defrauded anyone of anything, I will give back four times as much" (Lk 19:8).

Jesus' immediate observation was, "Today salvation has come to this house" (v. 9).

"Believe and Implore God to Save"

While the idea that men must plead with God for favors has been popular a long time, it has no validity whatever. In the issue of salvation, the matter is already closed. Salvation is available to those who claim it, and that's all there is to that.

As a result of Christ's redemptive work there is no need for the sinner to appeal for salvation or implore God to be favorable or gracious. If an item has already been paid for, one does not have to beg to take it, or pay again for it. We do not have to ask God to be what He already has demonstrated Himself to be—the Saviour of sinners.

It is encouraging to realize for a moment that the pre-Calvary prayers are no longer necessary. "God be merciful to me, the sinner," pleaded the publican (Lk 18:13). "Look upon me as You look upon the atoning blood on the mercy seat."[2] Obviously, these prayers have already been answered on behalf of everyone. The sacrifice of Christ has been accomplished and God is now merciful.

The Gospel asks sinners to freely accept salvation, not plead for mercy.

Would You Believe . . . ?

So much for the pure Gospel and all of its various amplifications. Clearly, salvation is freely available without ramification, direct from God, based on faith. Can you believe?

Believing a simple thing is difficult. While men have solved amazingly complex scientific problems, they have invariably stumbled over moral problems. Salvation has been elusive to many people because they are not accustomed to believing a simple thing.

Can you believe that Jesus came? That He died to bear your penalty for your sin? That He rose again from the dead to justify *you* (1 Co 15:3-4)? Will you trust His work of redemption (and *only* that) for your salvation?

Can you trust God to save you? Can you see that you're totally dependent on Him for this, and that you can never save yourself through your own efforts?

Can you believe the fact that God's salvation is free? Can you believe that faith is your only requirement?

If you can believe these things, will you now follow the instruction of Paul and Silas to their Phillippian jailer?

> **Believe in the Lord Jesus, and you shall be saved.**
>
> *Acts 16:31*

10

THE NEW YOU

If you followed the instruction of Acts 16:31, you're a new you.

You're a regenerated person, a saved human being. You're now rightly connected with God, and that's going to make all the difference in the world. And in the world to come!

You may have believed you had a right connection previously. You may have been morally upright, deeply religious, even a faithful member of a church, but you lacked "the righteousness which comes from God on the basis of faith" (Phil 3:9).

Some years ago the officials of a midwestern hospital discovered that the hospital's firefighting equipment had never been connected to the city water main. For thirty-five years patients and staff alike had trusted in the strategically placed hoses, polished valves, and the finest of machinery.

But there was no water. The pipe that ran from the building stopped four feet under the surface of the ground. No one had ever connected it to the main.

Fortunately the hospital experienced no fire in all that time. But they had based a life-and-death situation on a false hope. Had there been an emergency the situation would have been discovered too late.

So it is with the people of the world. The equipment they have appears adequate to cope with the natural environment, and it is.

But only if connected to the main. And so you must connect with God.

The problem with so much religion is that it is a *dead wire.* God is a live wire, when you touch Him, you'll know it. Others will know it, too!

Congratulations! You're a Saint

Now that you're rightly connected to God, congratulations! You're a saint.

The Bible describes the condition of saved people in detail and we can assure you that you are a saint, and more. The happy news follows in the ensuing sections.

You are not a saint because you have been canonized by a papal decree or chosen by some ecclesiastical council. It is not because some church has said so, or because we have said so. You have become a saint because God has said so.

In the Bible all Christians are "called as saints" (Ro 1:7), "saints in Christ Jesus" (Phil 1:1). God now constitutes you a saint (Greek, *hagios,* "a holy one") because you have trusted Jesus and His redemptive work, and the holiness of the Saviour has been imputed to you. God sees you henceforth only and always in Christ, the Holy One, accepted "in the Beloved" (Eph 1:6).

In that Christ has paid in full your account with God, the Father actually regards you as He would His own Son, "the Holy One of God" (Lk 4:34).

A saved individual becomes a saint positionally at the moment he is saved (1 Co 1:2). But of course his life will not reflect perfected sainthood immediately. This is rather a process to be realized experientially during a life of faith. As you fully realize what you have become in Christ, your life will reflect increasing sainthood in character and achievement for God, as well as in service for your fellowman (Ro 6:11).

Such a saintly life is not a matter of your own effort, however. You may well achieve the outward appearance of a saintly life. That, however, is far from the reality God describes for perfected saints. Actually, it is not you who will live this saintly life, but Christ living *through you.* You become a conduit through which Jesus Christ lives the sainted life pleasing to God.

Saintliness will be seen in you in proportion to how much you know and count on what you are in Christ. As you recognize and honor Christ residing within you, His incomparable life-style will be reflected out of you. Saints are earthly mirrors, in a sense, reflecting Christ to the world.

Saintliness, or Christlikeness, comes from occupation with Christ, not the self. "But we all . . . beholding as in a mirror the glory of the Lord, are being transformed into the same image (2 Co 3:18).

It is a fact of nature that human beings become like those they admire. Young boys and girls tend to be like their parents. In their games they emulate characters who impress them. Christians sing, "I would be like Jesus," reflecting the same tendencies.

But obviously, we can only be like Jesus in proportion to how much we understand Him and count on our placement before God in Him. A Christian saint must spend time in prayer, Bible study and contemplation of the Master in order to take on His characteristics.

In any case, regardless of how well you do at this, you are a saint with the full privileges of a son of God. Your commission cannot expire or be lost, and you can depend on God's help and guidance in your increasing maturity and Christlikeness.

Congratulations! You Are a Son and Heir

You have come into a large inheritance. You are now a child of God. He is now your Father.

The moment you believed in Christ you became a child in God's family. "But as many as received Him, to them He gave the right to become children of God" (Jn 1:12). "The Spirit Himself bears witness with our spirit that we are children of God, and if children, heirs also, heirs of God and fellow-heirs with Christ" (Ro 8:16-17). The term "children" (Greek, *teknon,* "one born") denotes those born into God's family through a spiritual birth (Jn 3:3-5).

While you become a *child* of God you receive, at your salvation, the status of a mature adult. Ephesians 1:5 characterizes your coming into the family as an "adoption" (Greek, *huiothesia*, "placing a son") so that you are recognized as grown and mature. As an adult family member you are not subject to the rules and regulations placed on children; rather you are given freedom. Grace, not law, is the concept of salvation.

It was Graeco-Roman tradition, in the New Testament times, to place a child under the guidance of a pedagogue or tutor to be trained for the rights and privileges of adulthood. This can be compared with man's spiritual childhood under the Mosaic Law of the Old Testament. But with the advent of Christ and salvation, the believer is placed in the family as a full adult, no longer under a teacher (Gal 3:25-27).

The adult adoptee is expected to do voluntarily what he would do under a teacher (or a law) (Gal 4:1-6). But even if he fails in this, the issue is not between the convert and the law, but between the convert and God, his Father (Heb 12:5-10; 1 Jn 2:1-2).

The Holy Spirit indwells all believers and assures the "son and heir" position through the believer's lifetime (Gal 4:6). As a result, the believer can live graciously, freely, and non-legalistically to the glory of God and the blessing of his fellowman.

But that's only to speak of this earthly life. The full significance and dignity and blessedness of sonship awaits a marvelous destiny in the kingdom to come, and through all eternity.

The full manifestation of the believer's inheritance awaits the resurrection and translation of saints (1 Th 4:14-17; 1 Jn 3:2). We will be taken into God's new order, and the full fruition of our salvation will be realized as we are transformed into actual conformity to the glorified Son of God, Jesus Christ our Lord.

The only earthly example that readily comes to mind is the incredible transformation of the lowly caterpillar into the lovely butterfly.

A knowledge of what's coming breeds joyous anticipation: "But also we ourselves, having the first fruits of the Spirit . . . groan within ourselves, waiting eargerly for our adoption as sons, the redemption of our body" (Ro 8:23).

We can readily understand Paul's enthusiasm in view of God's promise: "Things which the eye has not seen and ear has not heard, and which have not entered the heart of man . . . God has prepared for those who love Him" (1 Co 2:9).

Congratulations! You're Justified

The moment you believe in Christ as your Saviour God justifies you and calls you "righteous."

He does this because your salvation has stripped away from you the "filthy garments" of sin and self-righteousness. You are now clothed, as far as God is concerned, in the spotlessly white garments of divine righteousness, and you are acquitted of any guilt or punishment regarding your sins. You are justified on the basis of Christ, of course, and your earthly condition, good or bad, is of no consequence. You are justified by faith, not works (Ro 3:22, 28; 5:1).

This justification by faith, rather than human merit, is the heart of the Gospel, as we have seen. It is also the place which the enemy attacks most relentlessly. If Satan can cause guilt in a believer, even though none is ever appropriate, he can focus the saint's attention away from Christ. In Christ there is no guilt, no punishment, and no reason to be concerned about these things.

But it is a human tendency to worry about whether everything is alright, and the devil takes full advantage.

This particular battle of "principalities and powers," Satan vs. Christ, has already been won by Christ, but the great deceiver would have us believe otherwise. He persuaded Eve that there were things God was not telling her, and that a little taste of forbidden fruit would open her eyes. The same line today reads, "You can't possibly be forgiven, so come with me and I'll distract you from your guilt."

But there's just no point in our being concerned about our guilt or condemnation in view of Christ's finished work. True enough, we were guilty, but the penalty has been paid in full, and we are free and completely justified forever.

Congratulations! You Have a New Career

Now that you're saved a new career is open to you. You can yield yourself to God and obtain an important position in His work now and throughout eternity.

Every position in God's work is important, He stresses, and your help is needed. Your application has been accepted and the job is waiting.

You have the sacred privilege of making a momentous decision—to give your redeemed self back to God for His service. This is not mandatory; you may just rest in your faith if that is your preference. You will in any event be taken to heaven since salvation cannot be lost, as we have seen.

True though, rewards in the life to come will be based on the life lived here on earth. It is up to each man to yield himself as accurately to God's will for him as he can, and to bear his own cross willingly. The quality of your earthly life depends on your perception of, and obedience to, God's will.

But which of us, if called to rule, would not want to do his best? Congratulations on your new career!

Congratulations! You're a Living Sacrifice

Sounds like odd "congratulations." Who wants to be a sacrifice?

The apostle Paul expresses this request for personal dedication of the believers in the first person: "I urge you therefore, brethren . . . to present your bodies a living and holy sacrifice" (Ro 12:1). The language is that of exhortation, rather than stern command. Paul is not pressuring anyone. But why should the apostle have to pressure anyone into doing what is not only right but is the wisest and best possible investment.

Men sin with their bodies. It's an old story. But those who follow Christ are requested to forego these sins. And this, too, is a great privilege, very attainable under God's guidance. Such an act is "reasonable" (KJV) in view of the Son of God's sacrificing His own body for us. The "mercies of God" call us, as receivers of the results of Christ's sacrifice, to "present" our redeemed bodies to our Saviour. He died for us so that we may live for Him.

As one who has inherited His holiness (1 Co 1:30), you are called upon to live a holy life (Lev 19:2; 1 Pe 1:16). You are not to be conformed to the sinful ways of this world, but rather to be *transformed* by the renewing of your mind that you may "prove what the will of God is," knowing it is "good and acceptable—and perfect" (Ro 12:2).

The yielding of a redeemed life to God causes the mind to be constantly refreshed and renewed by God and His Word. Human thought processes, clouded and contaminated by worldliness, become clear and pure as a running brook.

You attain the position of not only being able to discern God's will, but being able to appreciate that it is your best option. It becomes clear that God's plan for your life is better than any plan of your own could ever be. You will be able to put it to the test and verify that it is superior. You will be like a storm-tossed ship entering a peaceful harbor.

Mrs. C. H. Morris exulted in the peace and freedom attained in following God's will:

My stubborn will at last hath yielded;
  I would be Thine, and Thine alone;
But this the prayer my lips are bringing,
  "Lord, let in me Thy will be done!"

Sweet will of God, still fold me closer,
  Till I am wholly lost in Thee.
Sweet will of God, still fold me closer,
  Till I am wholly lost in Thee.

Thy precious will, O conqu'ring Savior,
  Doth now embrace and compass me;
All discords hushed, my peace a river,
  My soul a prisoned bird set free.

The poet sees freedom in yielding to God in holiness. "Liberty in Christ" is spoken of by the apostle, even as he requests that we sacrifice our bodies. Odd that the New Morality, which we described earlier, speaks of the opposite as freedom; libertinism is given the high distinction of liberty.

The believer can readily discern which is true.

Congratulations! You'll Live Forever

You're never going to die. Congratulations!

You'll die a physical death, should the Lord delay His coming. But that is unimportant. He'll raise you from death at His coming. Or if you're living at that moment, you'll never experience physical death (1 Th 4:13-18).

It's hard to contemplate eternal life, but that is what God's Word explicitly promises us, and that is what we trust in. The details, beyond human comprehension, are in God's hands.

The long life that lies ahead will be a pleasant one, to say the least, in the very company of God. We have described heaven, where we all will meet some day, and we can understand the historic eagerness of Christians to see it all happen.

Think of it! Eternal life.

Congratulations!

11

A THING OF BEAUTY

If you've read this far you're probably a Christian. If you're a new believer, then this book has achieved its highest purpose—to be used of God.

If you're an old friend of God's, we still hope that you have found a meaningful message here, and we trust that information about our Lord never seems like "old stuff" to you. There has been a joy in writing this book about salvation, and we hope there is joy in reading it as well.

There is one more topic that rightfully belongs to any study of salvation, and that is the Christian walk, or experience. Everyone who is saved enters upon the Christian walk, and common experience has shown that it is complex and demanding—worthy of close examination.

Some seem to achieve more than others in God's service, but this is only based on man's observation. Our Lord valued the meek and the "poor in spirit," and in truth, He took more time in His brief earthly ministry with paupers than with kings. Truly, the successful Christian walk is a subtle inner experience which will only be adequately evaluated in the world to come.

What we say here about the Christian walk, then, is respectfully gathered from Scripture and meant to lend what it can to those already under God's blessing of salvation.

Deeper Spiritual Living

Surrendering the will to God is so momentous an experience that many have attempted to view it as something separate from salvation. In their quest for a deeper spiritual experience, they have sought "a second work of grace."

Actually, any concept of "second" grace reflects badly on the completeness of the salvation experience.

"The baptism of the Spirit" is another name commonly applied to some kind of extra blessing that follows salvation. It is a biblical concept, but is an inseparable part of the salvation experience itself, not something additional to be enjoyed by a few (1 Co 12:12-13; Ro 6:3-4).

Another difficulty in achieving a deeper spiritual life is the tendency of some Christians to seek at once perfect holiness or eradication of the old nature. The New Testament teaches, however, that the Christian position—dead to sin, alive to God—is that sphere in which God sees the Christian joined to Christ (Ro 6:1-11). That position is achieved in degree only as this concept is believed as fact and acted upon (v. 11).

Intelligent surrender to God is realizing what Christ has done for us and what we are because of it. He has provided us a position of being dead to sin before God, completely cutting us off from it. He has clothed us in His own righteousness and perfect holiness.

Yielding our redeemed selves to God to do His will for us (Ro 12:1-2) is the response of enlightened faith. We give ourselves to God because God in Christ gave Himself for us. We dedicate ourselves to God because we are in Christ, forever joined to Him in God's reckoning. We choose God's will because that is perfectly consonant with our position in Him who always did those things that pleased the Father (Jn 8:29).

Deeper spiritual living, then, begins with a clear understanding of our position in Christ—what God has done for us. There is a crisis of surrender to undergo, and it is a continuing thing, not to be rested in or to be at any time considered accomplished.

The continuous surrender opens up vistas of rich spiritual experiences which more fully define salvation. The significance of our initial surrender is realized as we grow in the knowledge of the Lord.

We realize, as we progress, that our initial moment of salvation had in it all the potential of a long and rich life. Implicit in salvation is a deep spiritual life, as the glorious flower is implicit in the seed, or the mighty oak tree in the acorn.

Justification, sanctification, and guaranteed glorification (Ro 8:30) come in a package with salvation.

Germinal in salvation for every person are all the glories and victories of a deeply spiritual life.

Turning over one's redeemed life to God simply allows the Holy Spirit to bring salvation into full blossom. As a florist arranges small buds in a vase to have the most beautiful effect, God arranges our ongoing growth and glorification. Our task is merely to submit. Our "working it out" just consists of co-operating with Him who does the real work (Phil 2:12).

Again, this continuous perfecting does not involve a "second experience" of any sort; it is merely a life-long experience of believing that we are what we are in Christ. Deep spiritual living is normal Christian living, attainable by those who are yielded.

The ultimate goal is incomprehensibly wonderful —our experience of glorification when we see Him and become "like Him" (1 Jn 3:2).

Have You Yielded?

This is the big question.

Yielding to God, like salvation itself, is each man's personal responsibility. And the fact is that many Christians have never really faced this big question. The issue of yieldedness to God and His will is some-times glossed over.

Young people particularly seem to find this diffi-cult. It is perhaps harder for them to surrender com-pletely; they are at a very self-directed period of their lives and they very much want to manage their own affairs. Their Christian progress runs into a dead end, however, if they have never given their redeemed bodies to the Lord.

Scripture indicates that God has a plan for each life, but it cannot be revealed to those who are not yielded to Him. Obviously they would not accept His plan, even if He made it known, if they were not yielded. God calls first for surrender, and then for service according to His purposes for each life.

I remember vividly how God dealt with me as a young man concerning the issue of yieldedness. I was saved as a boy of fourteen, but I did not come to face a crisis of surrender to God's will until I was twenty-four. It wasn't that I was completely unyielded to God during those ten years; rather, I did for God what *I* wanted to do for Him instead of what He would have me do. I went through high school and college, and even on to seminary, managing the affairs between God and me.

Through that period God was faithful on His side of the bargain. When I sought His leading or His will it was revealed to me at once. He most certainly was leading. But my specialty was choosing my own way and then expecting God to bless it. When it came to any showdown I was in full charge.

As a result, I experienced my share of defeat and frustration. God has a way of showing us who's Who.

I did not originally plan to go to a seminary, but rather to medical school. I planned a pre-med curriculum in college. God, however, did not plan on my being a medical doctor, and it didn't work out.

I tried my hand at song writing but my tunes didn't make Tin Pan Alley. Finally, I decided seminary was the proper course, and I began teaching school to raise funds for my tuition.

But when I got some money together I bought a sharp new sports car instead.

God certainly didn't sit still for that one. That car just never made me happy; I couldn't even sit in it, much less drive it. I finally sold it.

I enrolled in the Southern Baptist Theological Seminary in Louisville, Kentucky, and thoroughly enjoyed my first year and one-half studying with a fine faculty. But during the summer previous to my final year's study my life changed completely.

I had been satisfied that I was surely following God's will in my theological studies, but I would have been afraid of the question, "Would you go anywhere He might lead?" I was about to be forced to answer that hard question.

I attended the summer camp meeting of the Christian and Missionary Alliance at Mahaffey, Pennsylvania, that fateful July. A powerful call to discipleship was given there and I made a complete surrender of my life to the Lord (Ro 12:1-2). I promised God I would take hands off my life and leave the decisions strictly to Him.

I had the distinct feeling that something significant would result from my decision and I was bothered by inner concern about my studies. God wouldn't dream of interrupting my masters degree, would He? Still, I couldn't rest. I thought, "I've really asked for it!"

Some two and one-half weeks later I was in Baltimore at a youth rally, giving testimony of my surrender experience at Mahaffey. In the audience was a certain well-to-do Christian lady whom God had used to send many worthy young people to Christian schools. At the conclusion of the service she approached me and said, "Young man, I see the Lord has His hand on you. If it should be His will for your life I would be happy to send you to Nyack."

By Nyack this dear lady meant the Missionary Training Institute at Nyack-on-the-Hudson, New York.

I was impressed by her concern and kind offer, but as she spoke I was thinking, "Well, why should I be interested in a Bible Institute that offers no degree? My seminary will give me a masters in one more year."

But I was aware of another feeling welling up: Was God acting upon my surrender? Was this His will now being made known to me?

I was confused. I told the good lady, "I'll pray about it. Many thanks, really, but let me pray about it. I'll let you know as soon as possible."

As I prayed, it became obvious to me that God wanted me at Nyack. I just didn't understand it, I'll admit, but it was clearly His will, and I had just finished promising to follow His will, wherever it led, whether I understood it or not.

I assumed that one day I would understand that situation, and now, more than forty years later, I do. God set me on a path involving the change to Nyack and I have been richly blessed—far beyond what I might have even prayed for. The reality of my surrender was tested, and I'm glad I followed God.

A poem I memorized back then comes up often in my mind in connection with following the Lord's leading. I have long ago forgotten the author, but the message has always been with me:

> We plan and plan, then pray
> That God may bless our plan.
> So runs our dark and doubtful way,
> So runs the life of man.
>
> But hearken! God says, "Pray!"
> And He will show His plan
> To lead us in His shining way
> That leadeth in to perfect day
> Each God-surrendered man.

The God-Led Life

That day I surrendered my life—in August of 1933—I began to keep a diary. I have kept it ever since, and it bears wonderful testimony to the reality of God and what He can do.

The year I spent at Nyack was a wonderful spiritual experience. God's presence could be felt keenly in the natural beauty of the place as well; the lovely Nyack hills and the splendor of the Hudson, a sheet of liquid gold under the sun's glow by day, and shimmering silver under the moon at night. I was serene.

After Nyack, God led me to a pastorate in Buffalo,

New York, if you could call it a "pastorate." If the idea was for God to show me humble surroundings in His work, He succeeded. The church was a mere handful of people meeting in a small storefront hall in the Polish district of the city. But He had called me there for His purposes; the group had invited me and I had that distinct knowledge that this was God's will for me.

It's hard to write of the beauty of that place. Not because it wasn't beautiful, but that the beauty was in the eye of the beholder. You just wouldn't believe the glory that seemed to gild everything with God's presence in that modest place. The Lord transformed the run-down houses and old dilapidated stores, and the ugly became beautiful. It was like the soft snow that each winter transformed the unsightly old junk yard into a thing of beauty.

In time God provided our little congregation a beautiful heated and lighted auditorium in an ideal location. We rented it for three years until the Lord opened up a real church building for us.

In 1940, after serving six years in Buffalo, I felt a new leading from the Lord. The congregation had grown greatly and God had used our work there to save many people and bless them. I felt very satisfied. But I also felt that familiar call to move on.

"What's next?" I thought. I was open to another pastorate, evangelistic work, or further education. The last alternative was furthest from my mind because God had apparently already demonstrated that he was not interested in my attaining academic degrees.

But that was God's call, nevertheless. I had placed my earlier degree upon the altar—I had given up my masters for His call to Nyack. He was now returning my degree, and more besides.

I found only one door open to me—that of the Dallas Theological Seminary. I enrolled there in January, 1940, to study for the Master of Theology degree.

I was at my studies longer than I would have expected. God was preparing a wide ministry of writing and speaking for me, and He chose to lead me into much more study than I would have chosen for myself. I ended up with the Th.M. and the Th.D. degrees from Dallas Seminary, and the Ph.D. from Johns Hopkins University.

It's not always God's choice to give back what we have yielded to Him. In any case, He knows best. Looking at my life with the advantage of hindsight, I can appreciate that God did want me to study, but in His time, at His places, and to the extent He chose. One thing I can say for sure—I'm not sorry I surrendered.

One of my favorite poems describes my life more beautifully than I could do it:

> God wrested sharply from my hand
> A treasure—plan that I had planned,
> And bade me wait for His command.
>
> He overturned my aims for me
> And left me groping helplessly,
> Bewildered where I could not see.

Then like a blinding sun at night
He flashed upon my startled sight,
His plan for guiding me aright.

An untried path, an untried way,
A hitherto despised essay
Disclosed His will. Should I obey?

With heart depressed and secret fears
I took His hand to face the years;
Quiescent, but indwelt with fears.

To my complete and frank surprise
His way led out to shining skies
So bright that I must shield my eyes.

A pleasant way beset with flowers
A rock oftimes, but gracious hours;
With faith and love. His suns, His showers.

*What if He had not turned aside
My way for me, nor me denied,
But let me have my will to ride?*

AUTHOR UNKNOWN

Enough of my life. We should get back to yours. I can report my own experience of surrendering and attempting to follow God's leading because I am very familiar with it. I don't mean it to represent any example since we already have the best possible example in Jesus Christ. Also, it should be remembered, there are many lives lived better than mine or yours, for which God has chosen quietness and a ministry that

passes without public notice. He is "no respecter of
persons," as we have seen.

The Plan for Your Life

God has a plan for your life, just as he had for
mine. Assuming that you will yield to God, it's under
way.

Let's consider God as a planner for a moment. Look
at nature, and all His masterpieces, as the work of a
good planner.

He has a purpose in the sun, moon, and stars. They
not only adorn the heavens above, but they give light,
heat, and energy to the earth below, to say the least
of what they do. And their courses are laid out with
the ultimate in foresight and efficiency.

The clouds are not only a miracle of change and
splendor; they send silvery showers to earth for our
pleasure, and fleecy snow to bedeck our land with
magic artistry.

There is plan and purpose in the sea. God has set
strict confines to its sprawling majesty and ever-
changing beauty. In the day He created it as indis-
pensable to all life on earth, He limited its boundaries: "Thus far you shall come, but no farther; And
here shall your proud waves stop" (Job 38:11).

God has a plan and purpose in the mountain stream
dashing over the rocks, in the mighty river that
pierces a continent, in the babbling brook that graces
the lovely meadow. There simply is not a blade of

grass, a flower, tree, shrub, insect, beast, or bird for which God does not have a wondrous design.

That being true, how much more purpose and plan would He have for you, His masterpiece, a human being made in His own image? Man is the crown and goal of God's creation, and this is doubly true of redeemed man because He is doubly God's—by creation and by redemption.

Scripturally, God has a definite plan for each of His redeemed: "For we are His workmanship, created in Christ Jesus for good works, which God prepared beforehand, that we should walk in them" (Eph 2:10).

Each believer is spoken of as a poem by God, for the word "workmanship" may be translated "poem" (Greek, *poiema,* something made or created), the product of the skill and artistry of the Creator-Redeemer. Each saved soul is like an exquisite vase fashioned by the hand of the Creator. The original artwork, it is true, was marred and broken by sin, but God completely remade it. He "created" it "in Christ Jesus" more lovely and with greater potential than it could have had in its original state. He remade it for great usefulness in time and for tremendous glory in eternity.

The fact that God chose us in Christ "before the foundation of the world" (Eph 1:4) certainly emphasizes that He has a plan for each of us. The plan involves what He calls "good works." (We are saved, we should stress again, by faith, not works of any kind, but we are saved *"for* good works." We are to accomplish good works in Christ after our salvation).

What is most important to realize is that these "good works" which we are saved to perform are divinely "prepared beforehand"; God has laid them out for us. They constitute His holy will for our redeemed lives.

God's Plan Is Best

It seems too obvious to say that God has the best plan for our individual lives, but many Christians stumble on this point.

But if there is a Creator, and He made every creature, and He adapted each creature to His plan and each plan to His creature, there is just one conclusion. We sometimes forget in the complexity of our lives and our world, that God prepared the plan for us and us for the plan. Apparently all of our individual talents, worldly endowments, and personalities are taken into consideration and our plan is "tailor-made."

He foresaw how, where, and in what circumstances we could serve Him best, and He saved us to serve Him.

He who made us as His creatures (Ps 100:3) and remade us in Christ, can plan for us as no one else can. The infinite variety in human beings is reflected in nature as a trademark of the same Creator—no two snowflakes are alike; no two leaves, blades of grass, or flowers. Each has a purpose, with a design adapted to its purpose.

God's plan is best for you because it will bring the greatest glory to God. God has saved us to bring honor to Him, and it is a high calling. We will gather our promised rewards for our service throughout eternity, but we must serve now. We will serve as we yield ourselves. We will be called according to our willingness.

We can liken the phenomenon of salvation and God's plan for us to the situation of urban renewal, a hallmark of our times. In that situation, a designated area is set aside for the renewal, but nothing is done before an architect has made a detailed plan of the job. Everything is set down on paper before any work is done. When the plans are made, the old unsightly buildings come down and the debris is removed, depicting, in a way, God's removal of our sin. But of course the project is not accomplished with the removal, but rather with the installation of the fine new structures.

We can see in the illustration that the final beauty and utility of the renewal is largely the result of the architect's original plan. The builders are faithful to this plan—they "surrender themselves" in a sense. They do not merely proceed at will when they see an available space.

Similarly, when we are called up for "renewal," it is most essential that we remember to consult the Architect for His original plan.

Of course, discerning God's plan is not as easy as consulting a blueprint. This is no failing of the Architect, but rather that we are impatient builders. A note of warning is necessary here—God reveals His plan for each of us in *His* timing as *He* sees fit.

Sometimes we have to stop in our tracks and double-check where we are. Sometimes we have to be content to wait, and take no step until He beckons. God's plan, as many Christians have experienced, can be only partially embraced, or even missed altogether.

It is certain that a state of unyieldedness will cause the plan to recede from you. Disobedience will blind your eyes to it. Self-will will cheat you out of its blessing.

But the glory and victory possible with the Creator's individual plan make all amounts of patience and humility and surrender worthwhile.

Without a doubt, God's plan is best.

Discipleship

It is one thing to be a believer, and another to be a disciple.[1] Although even Christian leaders tend to confuse the two, they are distinct. A believer is a person who believes in Christ and is therefore saved (Ac 16:31). A disciple is a believer who has committed His saved life to the Lordship of Christ, his Saviour. He has yielded to God's will and embarked on God's plan for him.

Discipleship should always follow salvation as a grateful, spontaneous response to God's grace. We have already said that it is not a *condition* of salvation. That would be requiring the unsaved person to do what the majority of those long saved have never done.

The call to discipleship is as clear today as it was on the fateful day Jesus called the fishermen of Galilee: "Follow me, and I will make you become fishers of men." They followed Him at once (Mk 1:17-20), and His promise was made good in amazing ways.

He summoned the multitude with His disciples and gave them a thought-provoking message: "If anyone wishes to come after Me, let him deny himself, and take up his cross, and follow Me. For whoever wishes to save his life shall lose it; and whoever loses his life for my sake and the gospel's shall save it" (Mk 8:34-35).

Jesus probed the heart of Simon Peter, determining the extent of the disciple's commitment. Three times comes the searching question, "Simon, son of John, do you love me?" (Jn 21:15-17). Getting an affirmative answer, He goes on to prophesy the great extensions of Peter's coming ministry as an apostle.

The Lord still asks, "Believer, do you love me?"

Are You in Business for Yourself?

Whom do you serve, yourself or Christ?

We mean to draw a real distinction here because there is one. The Scriptures completely reject the idea of self-determination in serving God. There just is no such thing.

And this is the crux of the problem. Believers must subvert their own instincts, which they have been accustomed to following throughout their unregenerate lives, in favor of the commands of God, which might appear inexplicable.

George Fox, the founder of the Society of Friends, lived a remarkable life of self-abnegation and Christ-centered service. A biographer summed up his personal heroism in these terms: "The secret of George Fox's life is easily told. He was completely master of himself because he was completely a servant of God."

What is difficult to comprehend is that God will replace a surrendered life. In exchange for self-denial He gives a renewed conviction and calling. This has been proved in myriad Christian lives, but must be experienced all over again by each believer.

Many Christians are held back from real achievement for Christ by self-will and worldliness. They do feel the call to holy dedication of life, and they dream of conquest and glory for the Lord. But the requirement of true self-sacrifice seems to be too much. We all resist it, to a greater or lesser degree.

But we are all thrilled, and perhaps envious, to see true dedication. Lord Tenneyson celebrated this victory in his poem "Gareth and Lynette," in which a mother mistakenly tries to keep her son tied to her apron strings rather than allowing him to serve Christ. She urges him to remain at home, to "follow the deer," enjoying hunting and other domestic pleasures. But he remonstrates:

How can you keep me tethered to you—Shame!
Man am I grown, a man's work must I do.

Follow the deer? Follow the Christ, the King,
Live pure, speak true, right wrong, follow the King—
Else wherefore born?

The dedicated Gareth asks, "Why was I born, after all, if not to serve Christ, the King?" It's a cosmic question we might all ask. For what purpose were we born—and, more pointedly, for what purpose *re*born?

The scriptural answer is clear. We have been saved to serve. We have enjoyed double birth to glorify God and bless man. God gave Himself for us so that we may give ourselves to Him.

We can deeply appreciate now the report on the Macedonian saints in Paul's second letter to the church at Corinth: "They first gave themselves to the Lord" and then to dedicated service for God and man "by the will of God" (8:5).

Treasure in Earthen Vessels

A believer is like a plain earthenware box containing a fabulous collection of costly gems and precious stones. Men have discovered such treasure buried in caves, and Paul must have had some such figure in mind when he wrote that the body of a believer is to be compared to an "earthen vessel" containing the "treasure" of God's indwelling Presence. "We have this treasure in earthen vessels," he pointed out, "that the surpassing greatness of the power may be of God and not from ourselves" (2 Co 4:6-7).

People will not be tempted to attribute the remark-

able power within believers to their comeliness if they
are just earthen vessels. The figure pervades Scripture.

We "dwell in houses of clay" (Job 4:19), since
God made us from "dust from the ground" (Gen
2:7; 3:19). Our bodies are very fragile, easily destroyed like a tent torn down (2 Co 5:1).

Yet, how wealthy we are! The Holy Spirit lives
inside that very mortal and plain vessel. Thus the believer's body is a holy "temple" where God manifests
Himself. Weak and frail in all our stained humanity,
we become all-powerful with the Spirit of God in our
hearts.

We are debilitated and darkened with sin, but ultimately so wise and strong. Our daily lives show an
inconsistent and shabby testimony to our own efforts,
but what potential we have with God! God "has
shone in our hearts to give the light of the knowledge
of the glory of God in the face of Jesus Christ" (2
Co 4:6).

When we do yield to God, when Christ is able to
live out His wonderful life through us, people will
not see the homely earthen vessel. Instead, the life
will be opened so that the treasures within will show.
Unbelievers will be drawn irresistibly to what they
perceive as fabulous treasure, and rightly so.

Every man is made in the image of God and has
the perception to appreciate real treasure. The unbeliever is as struck with a fine Christian testimony as
he would be to find precious jewels in an earthenware vessel. We actually become the vehicles of
God's glory to draw others to Him.

Jewels don't spoil. They last forever. At any time, any believer may yield up that ordinary exterior to God.

And let the Son shine out.

A Thing of Beauty

Sin cheapens and degrades its victims. It makes people common and ordinary.

But when God forgives a man's sin and saves him, that man is changed. He becomes different from his fellowmen in the world. He becomes, according to Scripture, "a new creature." His testimony is, "the old things passed away; behold, new things have come" (2 Co 5:17).

The believer is no longer ordinary. God refers to him as "no longer common, but a thing of beauty." He is distinguished as a child of God, a saint, "in Christ."

Sadly, many believers do not realize that they have become things of beauty, and they tend to go on as if they were still ordinary. Many know their position in theory, but they tend not to act upon it, not having the faith to believe it will prove out as God says it will. They retain, in their conduct and everyday affairs, the typical characteristics of unbelievers, so that the Spirit has no chance to shine out.

The witness of many Christians is ineffective because the observer is able to draw no differences between them and unsaved people.

But the beauty within can certainly be translated

into action that is observable. Otherwise, it would be an impractical gift from God. Many unsaved people are initially drawn to the Lord when they observe something wholly refreshing about believers. Also, believers have truthfully testified to ultimately satisfying and victorious lives as the Spirit within is free to reveal Christ.

The watchwords again are faith and surrender. Faith is required to believe that God is really inside us, and surrender is mandatory to give evidence of Christ's presence.

"For to me, to live is Christ," said the apostle emphatically (Phil 1:21). "It is no longer I who live, but Christ lives in me" (Gal 2:20). He had achieved that transformation by which the common and ordinary became a thing of beauty.

Some of the most beautiful and skillfully ornamented palaces in Venice are made of common brick. The bricks themselves are made of ordinary clay. Visiting the extraordinary artworks the philosopher John Ruskin observed, "The best thoughts of their architects are expressed in brick. Shaped by their hands and set in their palaces, they are no longer common . . ." And he concluded, closely paraphrasing Scripture, that the plain bricks had become "a thing of beauty and a joy forever."[2]

Our Great Architect has accomplished the same effect with men, not bricks. Taking the ordinary clay from which He originally made us, He is able to render a thing of beauty, a joy throughout all eternity.

The Temple of the Spirit

Paul prevailed on the Corinthian Christians, people surrounded with the sin and immorality of a very worldly civilization, to separate themselves. They belonged to God, he said.

"Or do you not know that your body is a temple of the Holy Spirit who is in you, whom you have from God, and that you are not your own? For you have been bought with a price; therefore glorify God in your body" (1 Co 6:19-20).

The concept of God's ownership of our bodies is important to the Christian life. If we are to be properly yielded we must fully realize that we no longer own ourselves. Our bodies have been bought and paid for by Christ, and are thus rightfully His.

The psalmist reminds us: "Know that the Lord Himself is God; it is He who has made us, and not we ourselves; we are His people and the sheep of His pasture" (Ps 100:2).

Even unsaved people belong to God by virtue of their divine creation, but believers are doubly the Lord's, as we have said.

A little lad made a model boat once, and inadvisedly sent it sailing on a wide river. It got away from him and was lost. He was very sad, but by chance he recovered his boat. He saw it in a toy store window. The manager had purchased the well-made model from a stranger who had found it.

The boy was obliged to pay the manager's price to have the boat back, but he was glad to. He now doubly owned his boat—he had made it and he had bought it.

Obviously, God has gone through a similar experience except that His models tend to lose themselves. He still finds us and redeems us.

This involves a certain responsibility on our part with respect to God's commands. We cannot rightfully deny His double claim on our very bodies, nor ignore His preferences regarding them. We are not to go on living as if our bodies were under our own jurisdiction once God has paid for them. Our functions, positive and negative, faithful and sinful, are all His to manage as He sees fit.

In that our bodies are likened to a temple of God, we have a clear indication that they are sacred premises. Even a cursory glance at God's requirements for His past temples of Jerusalem will show that the requirements for purity and cleanliness were stringent. Sin in the sanctuary was unthinkable, as the very presence of God was manifested therein. Self-will was completely inappropriate in the temple, where explicit instructions of the Lord were carried out to the letter.

If we keep our own temples clean and unpolluted, solely dedicated to the high purpose of serving and glorifying Him, we will have the marvelous experience of Solomon, whose dedication of the mighty Temple was blessed with the very presence of God (1 Ki 8:10-11).

The Heavenly Artist

When a body is fully yielded to God, and kept spotless as He demands His temple to be, He can use it. And He uses it as a great artist uses the tools of his art.

He has a touch upon us that can only be likened to the touch of a great artist. When we truly yield our lives to Him, He can bring forth magnificent works from the least of us.

There is an illustrative story about the great violinist Fritz Kreisler. A wealthy English art collector had a rare old violin among his treasures, and Kreisler coveted it. When the owner refused to part with it the great virtuoso begged permission to play it just once. The request was granted.

When Kreisler tuned the instrument it was obvious that he was deeply moved by its sound. But when he began to play, all present were overcome. The masterly artist, combined with the masterly instrument, made music that simply overwhelmed the listeners, the art collector included.

When the exquisite concert was finally done, the Englishman stood enraptured. He watched speechless as Kreisler returned the instrument to its antique case as one might put a baby to bed.

Suddenly the collector blurted out, "Take the violin! It's yours!'" Kreisler was dumbstruck as the man went on, "I have no right to keep it in a case. It should belong to the man who can play it as you did!"

The reasoning was compelling. A fine instrument ought to belong to the master who can draw the finest music from it.

Likewise with our redeemed lives: God is the Master who can draw out the finest harmonies and melodies. Our lives become the noble instruments from which He alone can evoke all the latent music.

If we hide away our lives, as the fine violin was hidden in its case in the art collection, then the Virtuoso can of course produce no music. But if we say, "Take us, we're Yours," the music comes forth.

So, Christian, give yourself back to Him to whom you really belong. Let Him "play you" in your wonderful position in Christ. Let the world see Christ through you. You will be a joyful and radiant witness; you will know Christ genuinely and intimately. You will be extremely effective in introducing Him to others, not by what you know but by what you are.

God grant that you take this great opportunity now.

NOTES

CHAPTER 5

1. Augustus Strong, *Systematic Theology: A Compendium* (Valley Forge, Pa.: Judson, 1907).
2. Lewis Sperry Chafer, *Systematic Theology* (Dallas: Dallas Seminary, 1947), 2:197.
3. G. B. F. Hallock, *Twenty-Five Hundred Best Modern Illustrations* (New York: Harper, 1935), p. 85.

CHAPTER 7

1. Karl A. Menninger, *Whatever Became of Sin?* (New York: Hawthorne, 1973).
2. Fulton J. Sheen, "Emptying Heaven of God," *Baltimore-News American,* October 21, 1973.

CHAPTER 8

1. Lee Fisher, "Whatever Became of Sin?" *Decision* 14 (November 1973): 10.

CHAPTER 9

1. Lewis Sperry Chafer, *Systematic Theology* (Dallas: Dallas Seminary, 1948), 3:381-82.
2. See note on Luke 18:13 in the *New Scofield Reference Bible,* p. 1108.

CHAPTER 11

1. For a clear distinction between salvation and discipleship see Zane Clark Hodges, *The Hungry Inherit* (Chicago: Moody, 1972).
2. G. B. F. Hallock, *Twenty-Five Hundred Best Modern Illustrations* (New York: Harper, 1935), p. 89.